ROUTLEDGE LIBRARY EDITIONS:
WAR AND SECURITY IN THE MIDDLE EAST

Volume 7

NUCLEAR RIVALS IN THE MIDDLE EAST

NUCLEAR RIVALS IN THE MIDDLE EAST

SHYAM BHATIA

Routledge
Taylor & Francis Group

LONDON AND NEW YORK

First published in 1988 by Routledge

This edition first published in 2017
by Routledge
2 Park Square, Milton Park, Abingdon, Oxon OX14 4RN

and by Routledge
711 Third Avenue, New York, NY 10017

Routledge is an imprint of the Taylor & Francis Group, an informa business

© 1988 Shyam Bhatia

British Library Cataloguing in Publication Data
A catalogue record for this book is available from the British Library

ISBN: 978-1-138-19428-1 (Set)
ISBN: 978-1-315-54183-9 (Set) (ebk)
ISBN: 978-1-138-64766-4 (Volume 7) (hbk)
ISBN: 978-1-138-65543-0 (Volume 7) (pbk)

Publisher's Note
The publisher has gone to great lengths to ensure the quality of this reprint but points out that some imperfections in the original copies may be apparent.

Disclaimer
The publisher has made every effort to trace copyright holders and would welcome correspondence from those they have been unable to trace.

NUCLEAR RIVALS IN THE MIDDLE EAST

SHYAM BHATIA

ROUTLEDGE
London & New York

First published in 1988 by
Routledge
11 New Fetter Lane, London EC4P 4EE

Published in the USA by
Routledge
In association with Routledge, Chapman and Hall, Inc.
29 West 35th Street, New York NY 10001

British Library Cataloguing in Publication Data

Bhatia, Shyam.
    Nuclear rivals in the Middle East.
    1. Nuclear weapons — Government policy
    — Middle East
    I. Title
    355'.0335'56   UA853.M5

    ISBN 0-415-00479-9

Library of Congress Cataloging-in-Publication Data
Bhatia, Shyam, 1950–
    Nuclear rivals in the Middle East/Shyam Bhatia.
        p.   cm.
    Includes index.
    ISBN 0-415-00479-9
    1. Nuclear arms control — Middle East. 2. Arms race — Middle East.
3. Nuclear fuels — Middle East. 4. Nuclear nonproliferation.
I. Title.
JX1974.74.M627B53   1988
327.1'74'0956 — dc 19   87-33660

Printed and bound in Great Britain by
Biddles Ltd, Guildford and King's Lynn

Contents

For Amanda and Rupert

Abbreviations

AEC	Atomic Energy Commission (Israel; Egypt; Iran)
AEE	Atomic Energy Establishment (Egypt)
AEOI	Atomic Energy Organisation of Iran
AGR	Advanced gas-cooled reactor
ATR	Advanced thermal breeder reactor
BARC	Bhabha Atomic Research Centre (India)
BWR	Boiling-water reactor
CNEN	Italian Atomic Energy Commission
DCA	Design Consultants Association (Egypt)
ERL	Engineering Research Laboratories (Pakistan)
FBR	Fast-breeder reactor
HTGR	High-temperature gas reactor
HWR	Heavy-water reactor
IAEA	International Atomic Energy Agency
INFCE	International Nuclear Fuel Cycle Evaluation
LMFBR	Liquid-metal fast-breeder reactor
LSG	London Suppliers Group
LWR	Light-water reactor
MUF	Material unaccounted for
MW	Megawatts
NNPA	Nuclear Non-Proliferation Act (1978)
NNWS	Non-nuclear weapons states
NPPA	Nuclear Power Plants Authority (Egypt)
NPT	Nuclear Non-Proliferation Treaty
Numec	Nuclear Materials and Equipment Corporation
NWS	Nuclear-weapons states
PHWR	Pressurised heavy-water reactor
PWR	Pressurised-water reactor
SIPRI	Stockholm International Peace Research Institute
SWO	Special Works Organisation (Pakistan)

Introduction

'I am become Death, the destroyer of worlds' — J. Robert Oppenheimer on the first US nuclear test

The Middle East — one of the world's most politically turbulent regions — is the setting for a deadly nuclear arms race. Two countries, Israel and Pakistan, have mastered the technology for making nuclear bombs. Israel has the more advanced programme, including a stockpile of weapons, while Pakistan has only just achieved its breakthrough. The purpose of this book is to examine the evolution of nuclear research and development in these two countries, as well as the nuclear programmes of other countries in the region.

No Middle Eastern government has formally admitted that the purpose of its investment in nuclear research is to develop weapons. When questioned, the governments of all six countries surveyed here have justified their nuclear programmes by pointing to the peaceful benefits of nuclear energy, especially for the production of cheaper electric power. These arguments have less credibility in 1986 and 1987, as the price of oil has plummeted, and for oil-rich countries the justification has always been harder to sustain.

There are legitimate peaceful applications of nuclear energy, which were recognised long before the first nuclear weapons were designed. The central dilemma for architects of the non-proliferation regime has been somehow to preserve a distinction between the peaceful and non-peaceful applications of nuclear research. International efforts to prevent the spread of nuclear weapons are discussed in detail in Chapter One. The crisis of nuclear weapons proliferation has been especially acute for the United States, historically the most important exporter of nuclear know-how. The attractions of dominating the global nuclear market have repeatedly clashed with the dangers of allowing nuclear technology to be diverted for military purposes. United States policies, as we shall see, have had to take these contradictions into account.

1

An outline of the nuclear fuel cycle, which yields nuclear weapons material, is given in Chapter Two. Nuclear exporting countries have from time to time tried to restrict the sale of an entire fuel cycle, which would give importing countries the technological independence to produce material for weapons. An understanding of the fuel cycle is accordingly necessary in order to understand Middle East nuclear strategies.

Choices had to be made at an early stage regarding which Middle Eastern countries should be included in this survey. The criteria used were two-fold: the level of investments in building up nuclear infrastructures, and publicly expressed interest in all aspects of nuclear research and development. These guidelines led to the exclusion of countries like Algeria and Syria, which, although of undoubted political importance, have so far developed only modest nuclear programmes. Pakistan is strictly speaking not a Middle Eastern state, but its close affinity with the Arab world and the funding of its nuclear research by some Arab governments necessitated its inclusion in this book.

Nuclear rivalries in the Middle East are only partly a function of Arab-Israeli enmities. As the six case studies show, Israel's nuclear challenge did provoke an Arab response; but intra-Arab rivalry and notions of national prestige have been other factors contributing to the race. Iran's nuclear ambitions were fuelled by the Shah's desire to make his country the region's superpower. Pakistan, which accepted Arab finance, makes ritual gestures against Israel, but its nuclear policies have been heavily influenced by developments in neighbouring India.

It is probably not possible in the longer term to prevent the spread of nuclear weapons technology to the Middle East. More than 40 years have elapsed since the first nuclear bomb was dropped on Hiroshima and many more countries now possess the scientific and technical expertise to make such bombs. Determined governments, as Pakistan has shown, will always find ways of circumventing international non-proliferation measures. Industrially advanced countries can, however, slow down proliferation by restricting their appetite for nuclear exports, and the international community can ring the alarm bells when another country shows signs of crossing the nuclear threshold.

Nuclear research centres in the Middle East

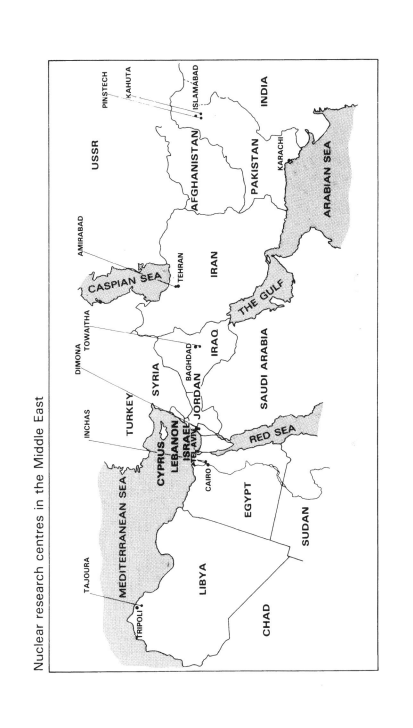

1

Nuclear Proliferation: The Framework of Risk

The double-edged utility of nuclear technology, for the production of electric power as well as for weapons, has been a cause for international concern since before the Second World War. Indeed, but for that war, when the Allied powers invested in a crash programme to surpass Germany's nuclear weapons research, the first nuclear power reactor might well have predated the first nuclear bomb, perhaps even excluding the latter altogether. However, the subsequent development of nuclear weapons within the context of the Manhattan Project in America, and the use of nuclear bombs by the United States against Japan in 1945, are now matters of historical record. So also are American efforts since then to control the spread of such weapons, both by voluntary renunciation under international control and supervision, and by negotiating mutually agreed limitations to weapons systems. More recently, American non-proliferation legislation has sought to strengthen sanctions against countries that were thought to be crossing the technological threshold of nuclear weapons development.

Historically, the failure of the 1946 Baruch Plan, which aimed at the creation of an international authority to control the mining, processing and development stages of nuclear technology, destroyed any hopes of keeping nuclear weapons out of national armouries. Later, in spite of rigid American secrecy after the end of the war, the Soviet Union, Britain, France and China managed to develop their own weapons stockpiles. In 1974 India carried out a nuclear test in the Rajasthan desert, although it claimed that this was for peaceful purposes only. Today more than a dozen countries have acquired the technology to make nuclear weapons at short notice. At least three, Israel, South Africa and Pakistan, are thought to have assembled nuclear bombs but not to have tested them.

International treaties that aim to control the spread of nuclear weapons know-how can at best be described as only partially successful. The Test Ban Treaty of 1963, which permits underground nuclear tests and has not been signed by either France or China; and the loopholes of the 1968 Nuclear Non-Proliferation Treaty, which again has not been signed by France or China, and which allows for the unfettered development and improvement of nuclear weapons systems among the existing nuclear weapons states, together with the halting progress of the Strategic Arms Limitation Talks — all these factors go to show that the nuclear weapons powers have not been able to agree on the restriction of the qualitative and quantitative spread of nuclear weapons — the issue of vertical proliferation — even amongst themselves.

Nuclear weapons powers apart, the spread of relevant technology has been so considerable that even poor countries with limited industrial bases have the means to manufacture nuclear weapons if they so choose. For such countries, moreover, the classical framework of weapons development, building first- and second-strike capabilities and sophisticated delivery systems, does not necessarily apply. Possession of a single bomb is held to confer prestige on its owner. Advocates of nuclear weapons development in poorer countries argue that even a few crude bombs, deployed in the most rudimentary delivery systems, may be enough to maintain a regional or sub-regional power balance. Terrorist groups using 'suit case' bombs would have even more limited objectives in mind.

This chapter is cast in the historical context of attempts to limit the spread of nuclear weapons. It concentrates on how political and technological trends, together with past economic forecasts, have combined to make available the technology for developing nuclear bombs in small or large quantities. A world of multiple nuclear powers seems almost inevitable. The risks of managing such a world, as well as new attempts to limit further proliferation, are themes for further discussion.

FISSION TECHNOLOGY

Uranium is the fuel in all commercially proven reactors in use at the present time. For all practical purposes, fission technology, which may be harnessed for electric power or for making nuclear bombs, is based on the exploitation of natural uranium (U238), which is not weapons-grade material, and its U235 isotope, which, if sufficiently enriched, can be used for weapons. A second uranium isotope, U233, has similar properties to U235, but it will be of practical use only when an economic method has been found for extracting it in sufficiently large quantities, possibly with the help of fast-breeder reactors.

As the chapter on the nuclear fuel cycle (Chapter 2) makes plain, U235 is found in natural uranium, but in such small proportions as to make exploitation almost impossible unless it passes through a separation process known as enrichment. The earliest efforts to develop enrichment concentrated on the gas diffusion process, which required very complex engineering skills and vast amounts of electric power. Gas diffusion plants still exist in the United States, Great Britain, the Soviet Union, France and China. Few countries have hitherto possessed either the industrial base or the capital to invest in gas diffusion for enrichment, but in the past decade, the development of new and cheaper methods of enrichment have made possible the production of U235 in many more countries. A more detailed discussion of these new methods follows later in this chapter.

The longer-term significance of uranium fuel is that it produces in the reactor, as a natural by-product, another fissile element, plutonium, which has value both as weapons-grade material and as fuel for breeder reactors. Any country with a reactor run on either natural or partially enriched uranium will find that it has also been made a free gift of plutonium, the quality and quantity of which will depend on the reactor's strength, the precise type of fuel mix on which it runs, and the length of time for which it operates. True, the plutonium, whether it is to be used as fuel or weapons material, must then be extracted in a chemical reprocessing plant. However, building such a plant is no longer as difficult as it used to be.

REACTOR EXPORTS

The prospect of using nuclear power as an alternative source of energy has long been discussed in international circles, particularly for countries like India, Pakistan, Egypt or Brazil, which were assumed to lack any significant supplies of fossil fuel. Where India was concerned, the first chairman of the Atomic Energy Commission, Dr Homi Bhabha, outlined a plan as long ago as 1957 for using nuclear power to meet most of India's energy needs by the end of the century. Bhabha's reasoning at the time was that his country had no oil reserves to speak of, and the resources of low- and medium-grade coal were sited sufficiently far away from the main population centres to make it both more economical and efficient to build nuclear power stations at strategic locations to meet increasing demands for electric power.

The pressing need for cheap and abundant energy in the developing world, and in the long term, even for energy-rich countries like the United States, was one factor in the prompting of an international reactor export drive, which began with the United States Atoms for Peace programme in 1955. Under this scheme, and in return for minimal controls, the American government gave small, experimental reactors to more than 20 countries in Latin America, South-East Asia, the Middle East and Western Europe. The aim of the programme was to demonstrate the peaceful benefits of atomic energy, drawing attention away from its military uses, while at the same time securing a foothold in the reactor market of the future.[1] This American experimental reactor export programme was followed and repeated on a smaller scale by the British, Soviet, Canadian and, most recently, French governments. There was an awareness at the time that such exports would make plutonium more widely available, but it was believed that, produced in experimental reactors, this would be in such small quantities as to be of no military value. Plutonium produced in commercial reactors, it was believed, would be 'denatured' and therefore not weapons-grade (a theory since disproved).

Plutonium contained in irradiated fuel rods would, furthermore, have to be extracted in a chemical reprocessing plant, a facility thought at the time to be beyond the capabilities of Third World countries. The Indian nuclear test of May 1974, based on plutonium obtained from a Canadian-built 40 megawatt (MW) research reactor and processed through a wholly Indian-built chemical plant, has conclusively proved otherwise.

In the 1960s and 1970s the demand for nuclear power stimulated the development of more and newer reactor systems. American companies and their European subsidiaries have dominated the market from the start with reactors of the light-water variety. A small portion of the market was captured by the Canadians with their heavy-water, natural-uranium-fuelled reactors (Candu). As the 1970s drew to a close, two new types of reactor systems held out hope of commercial promise: the French-built and plutonium-fuelled fast breeder, now actually in commercial operation in France; and the German-built high-temperature gas reactor (HTGR), fuelled by highly enriched, weapons-grade uranium.

The growth of the world market for nuclear exports has been accompanied by proposals among purchasing countries, notably in the Third World, that other key points in the nuclear fuel cycle — namely, facilities for fuel fabrication and reprocessing or enrichment — should also be available for export. The rationale behind these suggestions has been that economic independence from nuclear exporter countries can be assured only if entire nuclear fuel cycles are built within national boundaries. India justified building a pilot chemical reprocessing plant in 1964 on the grounds that this would provide valuable experience in making plutonium fuel for future breeder reactors. Similar arguments have been advanced at various stages in Pakistan, Iraq and Egypt. Pakistan, frustrated in its attempts to buy a French reprocessing plant, has since managed to build its own gas centrifuge enrichment facility.

ENERGY DEMANDS

Lower than expected rates of growth for energy consumption, coupled with higher capital costs for reactor building, have contributed to a shrinking of the world market for nuclear reactors. However, the costs and technologies of other elements of the nuclear fuel cycle have become easier to sustain. Countries that for the moment have suspended or reduced investments in nuclear reactors may, nevertheless, still find it attractive to invest in other parts of the fuel cycle that are now cheaper and simpler to develop. If nuclear power proves competitive in the future, these investments may in retrospect be considered worthwhile.

The single most important change in the nuclear fuel cycle has been the development of alternative enrichment technologies. Reprocessing plants have been within the grasp of most middle-range industrial powers for some time, but enrichment technology, dominated by the gas centrifuge process, has until recently eluded all but the five nuclear weapons powers. That situation has now also changed with the research and development of the gas centrifuge, jet nozzle and laser separation processes. The gas centrifuge process has merited the most attention in the world's press because of Pakistan's attempts to build its own gas centrifuge plant with the help of blueprints believed to have been stolen from the Dutch factory of the Urenco consortium. Even more promising is laser separation which, when it becomes available on a commercial scale, could be the least expensive and most efficient way of enriching uranium to whatever level is required. Brazil, despite the scaling-down of its nuclear power projections, is going ahead with plans to acquire an enrichment plant, although of the jet nozzle variety, from Germany.

INTERNATIONAL CONTROL MEASURES

The Nuclear Non-Proliferation Treaty

The Nuclear Non-Proliferation Treaty (NPT) remains the most important international attempt to prevent the spread of nuclear weapons. Final agreement on the Treaty was reached in 1968 and the NPT itself came into force in 1970. Its shortcomings may be summarised as follows: firstly, it has not been universally accepted, since two nuclear weapons powers, France and China, and dozens of smaller powers still refuse to sign it; and secondly, it creates a division between nuclear-weapons states (NWS) and non-nuclear-weapons states (NNWS), because the latter are required to accept obligations which do not apply to the former. In that sense the NPT is discriminatory. Furthermore, it does not meet the security needs of NNWSs. Countries wishing to withdraw from the Treaty may do so quite easily by giving three months' advance notice of their intentions. Still another criticism is that the Treaty does not prevent NNWSs from acquiring delivery systems or from developing weapons technology to such a stage that it would take only a few weeks to assemble and deploy credible nuclear weapons.

The discriminatory nature of the Treaty was criticised even while it was being negotiated. Several countries, including India, protested that it required NNSWs to give up the right to acquire nuclear weapons, while the NWSs were allowed to continue expanding and even improving the quality of their nuclear arms. The Indian delegate to the 1966 negotiations said this asymmetry in the Treaty reminded him of the Moghul Emperor who got drunk every evening but forbade his subjects to touch alcohol. Other non-aligned countries like Mexico, Nigeria and Yugoslavia made a specific list of demands for action by the superpowers. These included an end to underground tests, a substantial reduction in nuclear arsenals, a pledge not to use or threaten to use nuclear weapons against NNWS signatories of the NPT, substantial help in peaceful nuclear technology for developing countries, creating an international organisation to carry out peaceful nuclear explosions, and an undertaking to respect nuclear-free zones. It was in response to such demands that the Treaty was later expanded to include a provision requiring NWSs to pursue negotiations towards

9

disarmament in good faith.

Subsequent attempts to negotiate a comprehensive test ban treaty, the United States-Soviet Union SALT negotiations and the Treaty prohibiting nuclear weapons on the seabed, have all been cited as the NWSs' attempts to honour their NPT commitments. However, these moves have been criticised for being too little and too late. The NPT may nevertheless be considered at least partly successful because, with the sole exception of India, no NNWS has tested a nuclear explosive since the Treaty came into force. In this respect the NPT has undoubtedly been helped by complementary efforts to control proliferation. These include the setting up in 1974 of the unofficial Zangger Committee and its successor, the London group of nuclear exporting countries, to establish guidelines for exporting sensitive nuclear technologies, such as reprocessing and enrichment plants. United States legislation, including the Non-Proliferation Act of 1978, has also helped.

IAEA safeguards

Under Article 3 of the NPT, NNWSs are obliged to accept safeguards to ensure that nuclear technology for peaceful purposes is not being diverted to military ends. The safeguards have to be negotiated with the International Atomic Energy Agency (IAEA), which was created in 1957 in the wake of the American Atoms for Peace programme. The aims of the Agency are to promote the peaceful uses of nuclear energy under a system of safeguards managed by an international team of inspectors. While some have seen a contradiction between the promotional and policing activities of the IAEA, even more serious shortcomings are evident in the way in which it manages its safeguards. Safeguards are enforced by a team of inspectors who make a general survey of nuclear facilities to see if there is any evidence of weapons development. The team also makes an assessment of the total amount of fissile material that is being produced in a given country, with the intention of seeing if it can all be accounted for. There are, however, limitations to the effectiveness of such inspections. In the first place, the inspectors' team is still considered too small to carry out enough regular visits to the nuclear facilities of NNW signatories of the NPT. The Agency's accounting procedures, although now more streamlined, allow for shortfalls of fissile material within a given margin of error. The margin of error, or material unaccounted for (MUF), is now less than 2 per cent, but in large reactors and over a long period of time, it can add up to a significant amount.

Lip service is regularly paid to international strengthening of safeguards, but they still remain inadequate. Individual supplier countries have now taken to insisting on bilateral safeguards, in addition to those provided by the IAEA. The safeguards of the United States, Canada and the Soviet Union are said to be even more stringent than those of the Agency.

WEAPONS PRESTIGE

One proliferation issue to which the NPT does not address itself is that of the prestige conferred on nations possessing nuclear weapons. On the contrary, by reinforcing the division between NWSs and NNWSs, the NPT conveys the impression that nuclear weapons are a symbol of international status, which may even strengthen the diplomatic and commercial status of individual countries. By coincidence the five permanent members of the United Nations Security Council are also the world's first five nuclear weapons powers. In the long term, the prestige of owning nuclear weapons will only diminish if and when the NWSs seriously begin to disarm. Suggestions for the short term have been that the NWSs should stop meeting as an exclusive group. They should also accept international safeguards on all their nuclear activities, military and civil, so as to erase impressions that NWSs are in any sense more privileged than NNWSs.

In the aftermath of the NPT, discussions about non-proliferation were influenced by opposing schools of thought that may be said to have rested on best-case and worst-case scenarios. During the 1970s, best-case advocates, in which commercial interests were represented, argued that non-proliferation fears had been greatly exaggerated. Despite fears to the contrary, the number of nuclear weapons powers remained constant after 1964, with only one violation in that period — the Indian test — of non-proliferation concepts. Best-case supporters argued, further, that in view of the limited world resources of fossil fuel, it was both wrong and impractical to impede the growth of nuclear power, including the plutonium cycle, as an alternative energy source. The worst-case scenario, on the other hand, drew no comfort from the slow evolution of additional nuclear powers. Its advocates pointed out that the distinction between the peaceful and non-peaceful uses of nuclear technology was a false one, and such technology was so widespread that many countries had it within their means to make nuclear weapons within a very short time. For countries in this

11

category the actual testing of nuclear weapons was for the moment neither necessary nor important.

This reasoning led in some quarters to a complete reassessment of the value of nuclear power. The 'soft' energy school argued that nuclear energy was simply too dangerous to be allowed to develop further and was not economically feasible for many Third World countries. Furthermore, nuclear energy, especially for developing countries, was proving more expensive than originally anticipated. More attention should be devoted to 'soft' energy options, such as solar power.[2] Disincentives, possibly sanctions, could be applied against countries that nevertheless persisted with nuclear power programmes.

Other followers of worst-case scenarios said that the future did not lie in disincentives and 'soft' energy options, but lay instead in stabilising the effects of nuclear weapons proliferation. The superpowers could assist emerging Third World nuclear weapons powers, for example, by helping them to build early-warning systems, hotline links and good command and control structures. The effect of such assistance would be to reduce the risks of accidental nuclear conflict. It would also introduce a greater sense of stability and security.[3]

There was still another school of thought that resolutely refused to accept worst-case or best-case scenarios. Its exponents, whose ideological roots can be traced back to such post-war projects as the Baruch Plan, worked on the assumption that nuclear power would continue to play a part in world energy policies for many years to come. On the basis of this assumption they supported arguments for internationalising the nuclear fuel cycle by creating an international nuclear fuel agency and/or building multinational reprocessing and enrichment centres.[4]

Although such policies of internationalisation might indeed reduce the dangers of weapons proliferation, while at the same time meeting developing countries' fears that they stood in danger of being held in a new form of colonial bondage by the nuclear weapons powers, there were several possible pitfalls. These included the difficulty of selecting a particular country, or group of countries, to transfer the necessary technology of setting up, for example, multinational enrichment and reprocessing centres. The issue of who would transfer the technology, as well as pay for it, was not likely to be easily resolved.

From a non-proliferation point of view, any internationalisation of the nuclear fuel cycle only made sense if it also meant renouncing equivalent national fuel cycle facilities. Then again, if developing countries agreed to forgo the right to build national enrichment and reprocessing centres, would they not expect industrially advanced countries, including nuclear weapons powers, to do the same? The difficulties of resolving such issues was to demonstrate that in the longer term, political rather than technological issues lay at the heart of the non-proliferation problem.

UNITED STATES POLICIES — EBB AND FLOW

United States policies towards nuclear energy, and specifically towards nuclear exports, may be characterised as stop-go, or ebb and flow. As the Americans have been the world's largest suppliers of nuclear technology, their policies have a direct bearing on the nuclear programmes of countries outside the Communist bloc. They can make or break the non-proliferation effort.

Although concern over nuclear proliferation has reached new levels, attempts to institute some form of international nuclear control reach back to the closing years of the Second World War. Firstly the McMahon Bill, and later the 1946 Atomic Energy Act, tried to deny the export of American nuclear know-how until effective international measures had been established to prevent the use of nuclear energy for destructive purposes. Attempts to establish effective control measures were contained in the 1946 American-sponsored Baruch Plan. This Plan, which sought to establish an International Atomic Development Authority to supervise nuclear activities all over the world, could not be implemented because of irreconcilable differences with the Soviet Union. In any case, America's attempts to keep the secrets of nuclear energy within its own boundaries had manifestly failed by 1949, when the Soviet Union tested its first nuclear bomb. Britain followed with its first nuclear test in 1952, by which time both the Soviet Union and the United States had also tested thermo-nuclear bombs.

The failure of its earlier 'denial' policies prompted the American administration to change course in 1953, directly promoting the peaceful uses of nuclear energy. President Eisenhower's Atoms for Peace programme, which stressed the positive aspects of nuclear energy, aimed at exporting under safeguards nuclear technology for peaceful purposes. The drawback of the programme was that it drew too great a distinction between the peaceful and the military uses of nuclear energy. As the 1974 Indian test was to demonstrate, experience gained in running a peaceful programme can also be used to good effect for weapons development. One of the ironies of the Indian test was that American sales of heavy water helped to produce the

13

plutonium that was used in the explosive. In fact, the Indian test was not exactly a surprise for the international community. The 1968 Nuclear Non-Proliferation Treaty was prompted by fears that such a test was imminent and by concern that other countries might also be on the threshold of using civil nuclear programmes to make explosives. Although the Indians did not sign the NPT, the 1974 test was a set-back for the Treaty's sponsors.

There was acute concern the following year, 1975, when France revealed plans to sell a nuclear reprocessing plant to Pakistan, and West Germany announced 'sale of the century' plans to sell both reprocessing and enrichment plants to Brazil. Neither Pakistan nor Brazil had signed the NPT, and the decision to acquire sensitive nuclear technology, just as the Indians had done more than a decade earlier, inevitably aroused uneasy historical parallels. The French and West German deals also indicated how the United States was losing its domination of the civilian nuclear-power market.

It was in response to these new realities that US Secretary of State, Henry Kissinger, convened a meeting in London of the main nuclear supplier nations, the London Suppliers Group (LSG), to establish guidelines for exporting sensitive nuclear technology. The seven original members of the LSG, later expanded to 15, drew up the nearest equivalent to an exporters' code, although there were limitations to this gentlemen's agreement. Members of the LSG would not agree, for example, to a blanket ban on the sale of reprocessing and enrichment plants.

The fundamental reappraisal of US policy that began in the Ford-Kissinger years continued during the Carter Administration. In 1977 Carter, acting on the recommendation of the earlier Ford/Mitre Report, agreed to defer reprocessing for domestic and foreign needs. The Carter team, influenced by such experts as Professor Albert Wohlstetter, had identified plutonium as the key nuclear material from civil programmes that would facilitate the building of weapons. The aim of curbing reprocessing, as well as restricting the development of fast-breeder reactor technology, was to discourage the use of plutonium in national nuclear programmes. This new American attack on plutonium was reflected in the International Nuclear Fuel Cycle Evaluation (INFCE), which was convened in 1977 to take a new look at reactors and fuel cycles from a non-proliferation perspective.

Congressional initiatives

The fresh look at nuclear proliferation which began during the Ford years was matched by a series of legislative initiatives in the US Congress that were meant to buttress the efforts of the Administration. The Symington Amendment to the Foreign Assistance Act of 1976, amended in 1977, banned US military and economic assistance to any country that detonated a nuclear device, or imported sensitive nuclear technology without also accepting comprehensive safeguards on all its facilities. It was the Symington Amendment that provided the basis for Washington's suspension of aid to Pakistan in 1979, when the existence of a secret uranium-enrichment plant near Islamabad was revealed for the first time.

In 1980, following the Soviet invasion of Afghanistan, first Carter and then Reagan persuaded Congress to waive the Symington Amendment to permit the resumption of large-scale American military aid to Pakistan. Congressional concern that Pakistan had not ceased its efforts to develop nuclear weapons capability led to the Glenn and Cranston Amendments of 1984–5, which asked the President to certify that Pakistan did not possess a nuclear explosive device. Congress also attempted to restrict reprocessing, enrichment, fuel-fabrication and stockpiling through the Nuclear Non-Proliferation Act of 1978 (NNPA), which required NNWSs to accept comprehensive safeguards on all their facilities, in exchange for US technology. Some countries were also banned from reprocessing. A further provision required industrially advanced countries, including NWSs, to seek prior US approval for exporting nuclear materials or technology.[5]

The advent of Reagan

The Reagan Administration has been accused of retreating from earlier non-proliferation aims, but many of the policy changes introduced had their origins in the Carter years. The decision to renew aid to Pakistan, for example, despite Pakistan's continuing efforts to acquire weapons technology, began with Carter. It was Carter, again, who allowed US nuclear fuel to be shipped to India, although New Delhi refused to accept comprehensive safeguards. When US law forbade further shipments, Reagan allowed France to step in as an alternative supplier. Carter listened with sympathy to Western European and Japanese protests that US policies were likely to damage their commercial interests. Reagan later agreed not to inhibit reprocessing and fast-breeder reactor development in industrially advanced countries.

A Reagan adviser was to note that 'there is a fairly widespread impression that the Reagan Administration is somehow less committed than its predecessors to preventing the spread of nuclear weapons. This is not the case'.[6] The reason for this perception was a campaign remark by candidate Reagan that other countries' nuclear programmes were not the business of the United States. Although this was subsequently played down, the President's decision soon after to allow the post of non-proliferation adviser to lapse was seen as further evidence of a change in policy. It was true that Reagan did not give the same high priority to non-proliferation — he was more interested in strategic issues of East-West conflict — but his change of policy emphasis was also based on the realisation that the United States no longer dominated the nuclear technology market.

When Reagan relaxed the rules for reprocessing and breeder development, he was acknowledging the emergence of other industrially advanced countries that had self-sustaining nuclear programmes of their own with export potential. A senior State Department official recognised this new reality by stating that the US

recognises the need to make a distinction between those countries that are close friends and allies, and pose no proliferation risk, and those countries and areas in the world where we have real concern about the spread of nuclear weapons.[7]

Strategic concerns came into play with countries like Pakistan, which were a proliferation risk but were also seen as part of the front-line resistance against Soviet expansionism. The Reagan Administration did not encourage the export of sensitive technology to Pakistan, but nor was it prepared to penalise Islamabad for its clandestine efforts to make the bomb.

In many respects American nuclear policies have come full circle since the first nuclear bombs exploded in 1945. From the earlier policies of secrecy and denial, the United States then moved towards the active promotion and sale of nuclear technology for peaceful purposes. When the dangers of this policy became evident, the NPT and US domestic legislation tried once again to curb nuclear exports, except under strict safeguards, together with a threat of sanctions for violations. The non-proliferation policies of the Carter years were moderated by the Reagan Administration, partly because the US no longer enjoyed a nuclear monopoly, but also for strategic reasons. The restrictions that remain have come too late — so many countries have now acquired the necessary expertise that restrictive measures, such as the NPT or the US Nuclear Non-Proliferation Act, have at best delayed the emergence of independent and self-sustaining national nuclear energy programmes. Some of these programmes, as this book will show, have deliberately built-in military options that provide the basis for weapons projects. US policies and international laws will influence but not determine the final outcome.

The world economic recession and the energy glut of the 1980s have reduced the demand for nuclear technology. The disasters at Three Mile Island and Chernobyl have also dampened the global appetite for nuclear power, but the present lull is expected to be purely temporary, and a revival of nuclear exports is widely predicted for the 1990s. Countries that will then be in a position to sell their nuclear hardware will include those threshold powers, such as Israel, Pakistan, South Africa and India, that managed to evade the restriction of the 1970s. Their ability to export sensitive technologies will mean that the nuclear rivalries we witness today could be repeated many times over in the future.

NOTES

1. Steven J. Baker, 'Monopoly or Carter', *Foreign Policy*, 1975.

2. Cf., for instance. Amory B. Lovins *et al.*, 'Nuclear power and nuclear bombs', *Foreign Affairs*, Summer 1980.

3. Lewis A. Dunn, *Managing in a proliferated world* (Hudson Institute, 1 July 1976).

4. For example, J. Rotblat, 'Nuclear proliferation: arrangements for international control' in *Nuclear energy and nuclear proliferation* (SIPRI, Taylor and Francis, London, 1979).

5. Michael J. Brenner, *Nuclear power and non-proliferation* (Cambridge University Press, Cambridge, 1981).

6. J.B. Devine, 'The USA's nuclear non-proliferation policy' in *The international nuclear non-proliferation policy*, Simpson and Magrew (eds) (Macmillan, London, 1984), pp. 109–18.

7. Ibid.

2

The Nuclear Fuel Cycle

The nuclear fuel cycle is a term that incorporates the descriptions of several interlocking technologies, which have as their main purpose the treatment of nuclear fuel before, during and after the working of a reactor. Some reactors use highly enriched uranium (U235) or plutonium as fuel: the same material can be used for making bombs, and all reactors produce some plutonium as a by-product. For this reason the control of an entire nuclear fuel cycle, or at least of its most important sections — namely, the reactor, fuel-enrichment, fuel-fabrication and reprocessing plants — is considered indispensable for any nation that seeks to preserve a weapons option in its nuclear programme.

A typical nuclear fuel cycle therefore consists of the mining and milling of uranium, its conversion into fuel elements, the irradiation of those used fuel elements so that unburnt fuel can be reconverted for use in the reactor, with or without the plutonium that will also have been produced, and the storage or disposal of highly toxic and radioactive waste that will result in the reprocessing operation. A more detailed description of the fuel cycle follows later in this chapter. Not all reactors utilise the same nuclear fuel cycle: for instance, heavy-water reactors, that have been developed mostly in Canada, make use of natural uranium fuel elements in which the fissile isotope U235 is present in a proportion of only 0.7 per cent. Since nuclear bombs require uranium in which the proportion of U235 is very high, usually more than 90 per cent, the military implications of a heavy-water cycle do not become relevant until after the fuel elements have been irradiated in the reactor and later reprocessed for extraction of plutonium. Light-water reactors, on the other hand, work with uranium fuel elements in which the amount of U235 has been arti-ficially boosted, or 'enriched'. In this 'front end' of the fuel cycle the process of enriching uranium, before it is fabricated into fuel elements, is of military significance because it may result in making enough U235 available for bombs. Still another type of reactor, the fast breeder, produces more fissile material than it consumes. Here again, as with heavy-water reactors, the military importance of the fuel cycle comes into focus only in the post-reactor phase, the 'back end' of the fuel cycle, when reprocessing is required to remove the fissile material that has been produced in the reactor.

There are two types of fissile isotopes that are proven as weapons-grade material. All told there are three: uranium 235, plutonium and uranium 233. Out of the three, only uranium 235 is found in nature, although in such small concentrations that expensive and complex technologies have to be devised to produce it in large enough quantities. Both plutonium and uranium 233 are what are known as transuranic elements. They do not exist in nature, but are formed as the result of neutron bombardment in a reactor. Thus, uranium 238 (natural uranium) can be transformed into plutonium 239 and, likewise, thorium 232 may be changed into uranium 233. If exposed too long in a reactor, plutonium may take another form as plutonium 240. For a long time it was thought that plutonium 240 was too unstable for use in weapons, but a French test in 1978, using only 240, disproved this theory. Although Rutherford split the atom in 1919, research into building a complete nuclear fuel cycle did not really begin until after the start of the Second World War. This was because the idea of humankind controlling the power of the atom was controversial until shortly before the war. In 1932 Rutherford himself dismissed such an idea as 'moonshine'. Only five years later, however, in 1937, Aston reached the opposite conclusion. During a lecture delivered at Birmingham, he suggested that sub-atomic energy was universally available and one day, we would be able to release and control its almost infinite power.[1]

Then, in 1938, Hahn and Strassman discovered fission, and by 1941, British scientists had begun work on slow chain reactions related to work on their 'boiler' projects that were expected to demonstrate the use of nuclear power as an alternative source of energy. The credit for the first man-made reactor, however, goes to Enrico Fermi, the Italian Nobel Prize-winner of physics in 1938, who fled Fascism at home in order to settle down in the United States.

Fermi's experimental reactor, in which he was able to demonstrate the first ever self-sustained nuclear chain reaction, was developed in a laboratory built on a Chicago University squash court. Fermi's reactor went critical in December 1942, and it laid the basis for future research in the Manhattan Project, the American wartime effort aimed at building nuclear bombs ahead of the Germans. The Manhattan Project also financed the building of the first complete fuel cycle, a heavy-water cycle, which was to yield the plutonium required for the atomic bomb dropped on Nagasaki in 1945. Fuel elements were fabricated from uranium ore imported from the Belgian Congo. They were irradiated in reactors specially built for the purpose in Hanford, Washington, and they were later reprocessed according to techniques that had been developed by Glenn Seaborg and the Lawrence Livermore Laboratories in California. Indeed, it is arguable that the war stimulated the research and development of nuclear energy by making available large sums of money for projects like reactors and reprocessing plants that in peacetime would have been considered prohibitively expensive.

Without the war, research efforts would probably also have been directed more towards developing nuclear power for peaceful energy purposes. The British 'boiler' project, which had as its aim the development of nuclear power as a competitive energy source, was abandoned in 1941 because it did not directly contribute towards the war effort. However, in the words of one of the participants in the Manhattan Project, the early nuclear pioneers shied away from the idea of building nuclear bombs. Writing of nuclear research before the war, Dr Arthur Holly Compton said, 'In this hope there had been no thought of atomic explosions except as one of the hazards to be avoided.'[2] By 1942 the emphasis had changed to building nuclear weapons, first to keep ahead of the Germans, and later the Russians. As a result, civilian nuclear power projects did not gain ground until long after the war. Only in 1956 was the first nuclear power reactor for commercial use commissioned, at Calder Hall in Britain. In the United States the first commercial nuclear power plant was commissioned a year later, in December 1957, in Shippingport, Pennsylvania. A more successful version, which is still working, was commissioned in Dresden, Illinois, in 1960.

Manhattan Project scientists were concerned in the early years that enough uranium might not be available for their work. Fortunately for them, more than 100 tons of uranium ore from the Belgian Congo had been stockpiled in New York at the start of the war and this proved to be enough to meet their needs. After the war new reserves of high-grade uranium were discovered in Australia, South Africa, Canada and the United States. Low-grade ores were also discovered in India and Nigeria. The Congo uranium mines, which had been the main source of uranium supplies to Canada, Britain and America during the war, increased their production substantially. Nevertheless, fears about the comparative paucity of high-grade uranium continue to this day to influence national nuclear strategies. These fears have been used to strengthen arguments in favour of building plutonium and thorium-uranium 233 fuel cycles, since, so the argument runs, both plutonium and uranium 233 will provide valuable extra sources of fuel for future generations of reactors.

As uranium is the principal fuel required for current nuclear reactors, access to uranium ore is a key factor in any serious nuclear programme. By the end of 1980, global production of uranium ore per annum stood in excess of 500,000 tons. Between $400 million and $500 million is spent annually in uranium exploration, but controversy still rages over total world uranium reserves. An OECD/IAEA survey of 1977–8 estimated that there could be more than three million tonnes of uranium at a cost of up to $80 per kilogram, and a further million tonnes at a cost of up to $130 per kilogram. A subsequent survey concluded that there could be between another 6.5 and 15.8 million tonnes of uranium exploitable at a cost of up to $130 per kilogram.[3] These figures have since been revised and the price of uranium has fallen sharply. Most of the known high-grade uranium ores occur in sandstone and quartz deposits. Low-grade ores have been found in copper and phosphate ores, or else in marine black shales and coal. The world's largest deposits of thorium, which can breed uranium 233, are found in India and Brazil.

Uranium fabricated into fuel elements is lodged in a reactor that will produce both heat for electric power and plutonium as a by-product. In reactors dedicated to military purposes, mostly heavy-water reactors, the production of heat is an irrelevancy, since the main objective is the extraction of plutonium. Reactors themselves come in different shapes and sizes. They all have in common the ability to sustain a controlled nuclear fission chain reaction.

A brief explanation is necessary here to outline the principles of fission. Atoms consist of neutrons, which have no electric charge; protons, which have a positive electric charge; and electrons, that have a negative electric charge. The centre of an atom, also known as the nucleus, contains both neutrons and protons, with electrons revolving around them. A free neutron from another atom is sometimes able to penetrate a nucleus, which splits (fissions), releasing more nuclei and free neutrons. The additional free neutrons go on to split other nuclei in a snowball effect, generating enormous quantities of heat while so doing. In certain contrived conditions an unchecked snowball effect may result in an explosion. When controlled as in a reactor, the heat produced by the fissioning nuclei can be tapped for conversion into electric power. This is the controlled nuclear chain reaction. Not all nuclei fission upon being hit by a neutron. In some cases the nucleus may absorb the free neutron and convert itself into another isotope of the same element. In this way thorium 232 can become uranium 233, and uranium 238 will be converted into plutonium 239. The only naturally occurring element that fissions easily is uranium 235. Plutonium and uranium 233, which are artificially created, have similar fissioning properties.

The vast majority of reactors are run on fuel elements that contain both uranium 238 and uranium 235. Where the proportion of uranium is very small, as in natural uranium fuel elements, the reactor has need of a special moderator — either heavy water or graphite — which has the function of slowing down the speed of free neutrons, thereby increasing their chances of colliding with the relatively few uranium 235 nuclei present. Where the proportion of uranium 235 nuclei is slightly increased or 'enriched', light water (ordinary water) suffices as a moderator.

Besides graphite or heavy water, which have utility only in natural-uranium-fuelled reactors, all reactors require neutron absorbers. Shaped like fuel elements, neutron absorbers, often made of cadmium, are distributed in predetermined geometric patterns inside the fuel core. Their function is to keep in control the chain reaction, and they do this by being alternately raised and lowered into the fuel core. When all the control rods are fully lowered, they absorb whatever free neutrons may be in circulation and so effectively choke off the chain reaction. Water is the final factor in the make-up of a reactor. In reactors run on enriched uranium, light water may act as a moderator — in the same way as heavy water or graphite acts as a moderator in natural-uranium-fuelled reactors. Water also acts as a coolant. As it passes by the fuel elements, it collects their heat. This thermal energy is then used to drive turbines that in turn produce electric power. In some reactors — the British-made Magnox type, for example — gas, not water, performs the function of a coolant.

The most widely used power reactor system today has light water as both moderator and coolant for slightly enriched fuel elements. *Light-water reactors* are of two types — the *pressurised-water reactor* (PWR) and the *boiling-water reactor* (BWR). The difference lies in the way in which their respective cooling systems are constructed. The PWR's coolant circulates in two coils or loops. In the first loop the water is pressurised so that water is not allowed to boil. Heat is exchanged with the secondary loop, in which water circulates at a lower pressure outside the reactor vessel, which produces the steam required for the turbines. In BWRs, the coolant circulates inside a single loop and comes to a boil immediately after leaving the core, but while still inside the reactor vessel. After leaving the turbines, the steam comes into contact with a heat condenser and is converted back into water for use once more as a coolant. The *pressurised heavy-water reactor* (PHWR) is constructed along the same principles as the PWR. The difference lies in the fuel elements, made of natural uranium, and the need for heavy water as moderator and sometimes also as coolant.

Canada is the country most closely associated with the commercial success of PHWRs (the Candu PHWR), but other countries, notably France and Britain, are also interested in this technology. The Canadians have had the most commercial success in marketing their Candu PHWRs, but using natural uranium as fuel for power reactors was first demonstrated in Britain. Calder Hall,[4] the 182 MW reactor that went critical in 1956, was run on natural uranium fuel. However, British scientists chose to use graphite as a moderator, instead of heavy water, and carbon dioxide gas as a coolant. Calder Hall was the prototype for the first generation of such nuclear power reactors that became colloquially known as Magnox reactors because their natural uranium fuel was enclosed in a magnesium alloy cladding.

For the subsequent generation of reactors, the British chose an advanced version of the same Magnox-type reactors, also operating on slightly enriched uranium fuel, with graphite for a moderator and carbon dioxide again as the coolant. The fuel used was ceramic UO_2 instead of uranium metal. The cladding, instead of being Magnox, was stainless steel. As a result the advanced gas-cooled reactors (AGRs), as they became known in Britain, were able to operate at high temperatures without any danger of the fuel cladding melting. In West Germany and the United States, the British experience with AGRs was still further refined to develop the *high-temperature gas reactor* (HTGR), in which the gas coolant used is helium rather than carbon dioxide. The HTGR uses highly enriched uranium (93 per cent) and thorium as fuel. During reactor operations the thorium converts into uranium 233 for use in future fuel combinations.

Although fissile material is produced in all LWRs, PHWRs and HTGRs, there has been considerable international interest in designing a reactor in which the fissile yield would be greater than is possible in existing power reactors. One new concept researched in the United States is the advanced thermal breeder reactor (ATR), based on the PWR design. The difference lies in the composition of the fuel core. In ATRs the fuel core is comprised of a mix of uranium and thorium, surrounded by a thorium blanket. During reactor operations, neutrons leaking from the core fertilise the thorium blanket and change it into uranium 233. ATRs are designed to produce as much fissile material as they consume in the fuel core, but larger quantities of plutonium or uranium 233 are possible only with fast-breeder reactors (FBRs), which produce more fissile material than they consume.

FBRs are different from ATRs in the design of both fuel core and cooling systems. In the plutonium FBR, no moderator is present to slow down the neutrons emitted from a fuel core of highly enriched uranium and plutonium. Neutrons from the core go on to fertilise a surrounding blanket of uranium 238 that duly converts to plutonium. In the thorium breeder, an enriched uranium-thorium core, also without a moderator, is surrounded by a thorium 232 blanket that changes to uranium 233. The preferred coolant in most FBRs is liquid sodium, because of its low moderating qualities — hence the sometimes-used name, *liquid-metal fast-breeder reactor* (LMFBR). The reasoning behind the development of ATRs and FBRs springs from international concern to build up adequate stocks of plutonium and uranium 233 as alternative nuclear fuels. If the FBRs were developed in the United States they would be able to draw on the huge reserves of depleted natural uranium fuels already in existence from previous reactor generations, that are expected to breed enough plutonium for generations to come.

FRONT END OF THE FUEL CYCLE

The fuel cycle of all reactor systems begins with the mining and milling of uranium, which contains two isotopes: the fertile isotope uranium 238, that may later be converted into plutonium, and the less-abundant fissile isotope, uranium 235. Most uranium deposits are low-grade and uranium extraction is the by-product of other mining operations associated with, for example, copper, gold or phosphates. High-grade uranium ores found in sandstone and quartz-type deposits are located in North America, Australia and Africa. Thorium, which has a role to play in some fuel cycles, is more abundant. Vast deposits are located among the black sands of south-west India and also in the Egyptian delta. Some deposits are also known to exist randomly in veins and sedimentary rocks in other parts of the world.

Uranium ore fresh from the mine contains many impurities, which have to be removed before the ore is fabricated into fuel. After mechanical and chemical processing at a uranium mill, often located very close to the site of the mine, the ore is refined to a uranium ore concentrate called 'yellow cake', which contains between 70 and 90 per cent uranium oxide (U_3O_8). If the intention is to make fuel for PHWRs, the yellow cake itself provides the basis for fabrication into fuel elements. For other reactor systems the production of yellow cake is only the first step in a much longer process.

Conversion and enrichment

As the concentration of uranium 235 is so low, most power reactors, with the exception of PHWRs, require some degree of uranium enrichment. To begin with, yellow cake is converted to a uranium gaseous compound, uranium hexafluoride (UF_6), also known as hex. Conversion of UF_6 is a technological prerequisite for all subsequent methods of enrichment. It is as well to remember that since enrichment provides a direct route to weapons-grade uranium, such technology falls within a highly classified category. Traditionally, enrichment technology has been regarded as expensive, complex and energy-guzzling. Huge amounts of electricity are required to sustain the operation of any given enrichment plant. However, advances within this field — for instance, in developing gas centrifuges — have reduced overall costs and brought the technology nearer the grasp of developing countries with limited industrial bases.

The five known nuclear weapons powers have all built their own enrichment facilities. India, sometimes referred to as the sixth nuclear power after it tested a so-called peaceful nuclear device in 1974, chose the reprocessing route to procure the fissile material for its test. Pakistan is developing both reprocessing and enrichment plants for its nuclear programme. South Africa is believed to have finished building its enrichment plant, and Brazil is building one of its own in collaboration with West Germany. Besides these national enrichment facilities for domestic uses, and in keeping with the spirit of the Nuclear Non-Proliferation Treaty, individual governments are sometimes able to offer the use of their enrichment services for research and power reactors to countries that have signed the NPT and are willing to accept IAEA safeguards. Multinational enrichment consortia like Urenco and Eurodif are also able to offer enrichment services on similar terms.

Research into enrichment technologies is concentrating on four areas of promise. They are the gaseous diffusion, gas centrifuge, aerodynamic and laser processes. The objective of each individual process is to improve on the cost-effectiveness of increasing the concentration of uranium 235 to between 2 per cent and sometimes more than 90 per cent. As we have seen, all reactors, with the exception of PHWRs, require enriched uranium fuel to a lesser or greater degree. The amount of enrichment required ranges from 2–4 per cent for light-water reactors (LWRs), to more than 90 per cent for HTGRs.

Gaseous diffusion

Enrichment by gaseous diffusion is the oldest and best-known technique. The five nuclear weapons powers, the United States, the Soviet Union, Britain, France and China, either have had or still maintain diffusion plants to supply the enriched uranium required for power plants as well as for nuclear warheads. The diffusion process itself consists of taking gaseous hex and passing it through fine, porous membranes. Hex containing lighter UF_6 molecules, made up of uranium 235, passes more quickly through the membranes than do the heavier molecules containing uranium 238. In this way as the hex passes through successive membrane barriers, and several thousand such barriers are required, the required degree of uranium enrichment is achieved. Since the diffusion process is expensive in terms of both money and energy consumption, research continues for developing other types of enrichment techniques.

Gas centrifuge

Among the more promising alternatives to diffusion is gas centrifuge technology that has been developed jointly by Britain, West Germany and Holland in the Urenco consortium. A centrifuge plant is already in operation in Britain and two others are being constructed in West Germany and Holland. Considerable publicity has attached itself to the development of this technique because of its smaller capital costs and relatively low consumption of energy. The Urenco model is believed to be the basis on which Pakistan is developing its own enrichment programme.[5] As its name suggests, this technology is based on the principle of using centrifugal forces to separate the light and heavy molecules contained in hex. Hex is repeatedly fed through successive groups of centrifuges, all operating at very high speeds and built in units known as cascades. A single centrifuge cascade may contain

26

as many as a thousand centrifuges, sometimes more.

Aerodynamic methods

These incorporate the jet nozzle and Becker diffusion processes, which have been developed at the nuclear research centre at Karlsruhe, West Germany, and also in South Africa. Here again centrifugal forces are utilised to separate light from heavy molecules. However, the feed mixture consists of both hex and hydrogen, which are pumped at high pressure along a semicircular route. Both capital costs and energy consumption levels are thought to be much lower than for gaseous diffusion. A massive deal has been signed by West Germany to establish aerodynamic diffusion plants in Brazil.

Laser separation

Although still in the experimental stage, laser separation offers the prospect of being the most effective and least expensive method of enriching uranium. Laser beams are used to agitate or excite one of the two uranium isotopes. So effective is this method that it could in theory achieve as much as 50 per cent enrichment in a single stage. Another advantage is that lasers could be effectively used to extract uranium 235 in the depleted or left-over uranium stockpiles that have accumulated at the sites of the world's major enrichment plants. Gaseous diffusion plants alone, the longest-established enrichment units, have huge stocks of left-over uranium that would provide a rich source of unused uranium 235 to be extracted by laser technology.

Fuel fabrication

The technology for making nuclear fuel elements is constructed according to the needs of different reactor types. In PHWRs, the fabrication of fuel elements begins with the conversion of yellow cake into uranium oxide powder (UO_2). In light-water reactors (LWRs) the feed material is enriched hex. The uranium dioxide powder is then shaped and pressed into pellets, which are in turn packed into long, tube-shaped fuel rods made of either zircaloy or whatever other cladding material is considered suitable.[6] Individual fuel rods are arranged together in units called fuel assemblies, or fuel bundles, which make up the fuel core of the reactor. Strict quality control is applied throughout the mechanical processing of uranium dioxide into fuel pellets and beyond to remove any chemical impurities in the pellets, as well as to test for stresses and strains in the fuel cladding. The types of tests used may include X-rays, ultrasonic beams and chemical analysis.

International experience in fuel fabrication has been largely, but not exclusively, confined to the production of uranium fuels. There has also been research and development in the production of thorium-bearing fuels as well as mixed oxide fuels that include plutonium. In both such cases the experience gained is invaluable for its application in the production of fuel cores for breeder reactors.

BACK END OF THE FUEL CYCLE

The back end of the fuel cycle describes the handling of fuel elements after they have been irradiated or 'burnt' inside a reactor. Highly radioactive wastes, as well as toxic by-products like plutonium, are contained inside used fuel elements. A first step, therefore, is the safe storage of such elements by remote control until they are 'cool' and the most intense radioactivity has died down. This is accomplished by storing the used fuel elements either in the pool of the reactor vessel itself, or else in specially designed cooling ponds near the reactor site. Thereafter, the elements can either be disposed of as they are, waste, plutonium and all — this is known as the 'once through strategy' — or else undergo chemical reprocessing in order to remove unburnt uranium and plutonium for future use. As is the case with enrichment plants, reprocessing plants, because they extract plutonium, provide a route to weapons-grade fissile material.

Information about such plants is accordingly difficult to obtain. Enough, however, is known from open literature for a number of countries to try to build their own reprocessing technology. Among developing countries, India was the first to build a pilot, and later major, reprocessing plant from its own resources and freely available literature. Pakistan is building pilot-scale reprocessing facilities; so also is Argentina. Israel is thought to have had laboratory-scale reprocessing experience going back at least a decade.

REPROCESSING

The history of reprocessing is connected with wartime objectives of obtaining plutonium for use in nuclear warheads. Early reprocessing was therefore confined only to military reactors. It was extended only later to civilian reactors when fears grew about the limited availability of uranium. Strategies were then evolved for building up plutonium stocks so that alternative nuclear fuels might be available when global reserves of uranium dried up.

The used fuel elements of a typical PWR are estimated to contain 96 per cent uranium, 1 per cent plutonium and 3 per cent of radioactive fission fragments.[7] When the most intense radioactivity of these fragments has died down, a minimum period of 150 days, the fuel can be transferred in specially shielded casks to the reprocessing plant. Once inside the plant, the fuel is processed by both mechanical and chemical means. The mechanical steps necessary involve the chopping or shredding of fuel rods, their immersion in a solution of nitric acid and the subsequent separation of uranium, plutonium and radioactive waste by organic solvent extraction. Recovered uranium may be converted back into hex, for refabricating into fuel, plutonium can be converted into plutonium dioxide (PuO_2) for mixed oxide fuel elements, or else into metal form for military uses, and different levels of treatment are applied to the residual waste.

Reprocessing techniques which extract uranium and plutonium, and dispose of nuclear waste separately, are known as the Purex method of reprocessing. Another method, the Civex technique, does not separate plutonium entirely from radioactive fission waste.[8] As a result the plutonium is too 'hot' to handle for years to come. Although it has its limitations for the present, Civex has been cited as one way of limiting weapons proliferation risks in civilian reactors, since the plutonium yield is too 'hot' with radioactivity and therefore too dangerous to manage in any clandestine mid-way diversion for military use. Another reprocessing technique, Thorex, has been designed to reprocess thorium fuels, containing uranium 233, from HTGRs, ATRs and fast breeders.

WASTE MANAGEMENT

The management and disposal of nuclear waste constitute the final section of the fuel cycle. Radioactive waste is formed at every step of the fuel cycle and individual radioactive products have half-lives ranging from a few microseconds to several thousand years. Most of such products are contained in used fuel elements. They are usually in gaseous or liquid form and can be disposed of relatively painlessly. *Low-level waste* may be buried in shallow trenches on land, or else dumped into the ocean. If it is in gaseous form, it is released in small quantities into the atmosphere from the chimney-type stacks of the reprocessing plant. *Medium- and high-level waste*, which contain radioactive products with longer half-lives, may be temporarily stored or else solidified until a decision is reached about permanent disposal. For high-level waste the favoured disposal method is first to have it vitrified (glassified), then placed in specially designed lead containers which are in turn buried in stable geological formations, for instance in disused salt mines. Other suggested methods for disposal that have been discussed in the past include shooting high-level waste into outer space, or else dumping the lead containers into some deep ocean trough. Such alternatives are at present considered to bear too high a failure risk.

Even if all reprocessing efforts were to be halted, radioactive fission products would still remain inside the burnt fuel elements that are at present stored in or around various reactor sites all over the world. Since existing cooling ponds have a finite capacity for storing used fuel elements, the issue of burnt fuel management and waste disposal is of critical international importance.

A SUMMARY OF DIFFERENT FUEL CYCLES

The overwhelming majority of reactors in use today depend on one of two fuel cycles. These are:

(a) *The natural uranium fuel cycle*. Reactors using natural uranium as fuel are either PHWRs, like Candu, which employ heavy water as a moderator, or Magnox, which have graphite moderators and gas coolants.

(b) *Slightly enriched uranium fuel cycle*. Both PWRs and BWRs are run on slightly enriched uranium fuel. Light water is used as a moderator and coolant in both cases.

For both types of fuel cycles a further decision has to be made about whether to reprocess burnt fuel for future use, or else to dispose of it once it comes out of the reactor. If there is no intention to reprocess used fuel elements, the fuel cycle is guided by a 'once-through strategy.` Uranium is mined, milled, enriched (for LWRs), fabricated into fuel elements, irradiated inside a reactor, stored in cooling ponds after being used inside the reactor, and later disposed of in whatever way is considered suitable.

If the intention is to reprocess burnt fuel in order to extract uranium and plutonium for future civilian or military use, the fuel cycle is said to have a recycling objective. Here, burnt fuel is removed from the reactor, temporarily stored in cooling ponds and later sent to a chemical reprocessing plant where depleted uranium dioxide and plutonium are separated from radioactive fission fragments. Plutonium dioxide may later be combined with uranium dioxide to form pellets which can be used as mixed oxide fuel, while the depleted uranium oxide is converted back into hex, which is re-enriched before being fabricated once more into fuel.

Although plutonium extracted from recycling may be used in mixed oxide fuels for LWRs and PHWRs, it is also relevant for FBRs. In FBRs the fuel core consists of slightly enriched uranium and plutonium, which is surrounded by a blanket of natural uranium. During reactor operations, part of the fuel core, as well as the surrounding blanket, is converted into plutonium. Fast breeders and other advanced reactor systems may also be adapted to use thorium for conversion into uranium 233. International interest in the thorium-uranium fuel cycle stems from the huge known global deposits of thorium and also because uranium 233, which is bred from thorium, is less toxic than plutonium.

Thorium-uranium fuel cycle

The thorium-uranium fuel cycle can be adapted for use in FBRs, HTGRs and ATRs. For HTGRs the fuel cycle strategy begins with the mining and milling of uranium, its conversion into hex and enrichment to more than 90 per cent. Thorium is also mined, refined and combined with uranium in the fuel core. During reactor operations, the thorium fuel elements are converted into uranium 233. Burnt reactor fuel must then be reprocessed for extraction of uranium 233. In FBRs the same principle applies, although the uranium-thorium fuel core is also surrounded by a thorium blanket. Both the fuel core and the blanket are later pregnant with uranium 233, which may be extracted in a reprocessing plant.

Fuel cycle options

Although great strides have been made in the research and development of fast breeders, most advanced reactor systems are still to be commercially proven. For developing countries especially, where applied nuclear research is still in its infancy, the choice boils down to choosing between reactors using the enriched uranium or natural uranium fuel cycle. The choice of a natural-uranium fuel cycle means opting for PHWRs, almost certainly the Canadian Candu reactor, since the British AGR is not for sale. India, too, has hopes of developing its own Candu-type system, but commercial production is still a long way off and its own domestic needs are too great for any export possibilities in the near future.

The great advantage of PHWRs is the prospect they provide of fuel cycle independence. Any country with reasonable deposits of uranium ore could fabricate its own fuel elements without having to worry about future changes in the exporting policy of a supplier country. This was one of the reasons why India chose the PHWR for its first generation of nuclear power reactors. Similar considerations have influenced Argentina and Pakistan in their choice of power reactors, and also PHWRs. The mining of natural uranium, its processing into yellow cake and subsequent conversion into fuel elements still require some basic scientific and technological know-how. A fuel-fabrication plant will also need metallurgical and engineering skills of some sophistication. However, these technologies are not within the classified category and, as Pakistan has most recently demonstrated, even countries with a small industrial base can acquire them without too much difficulty. Reprocessing and enrichment plants, by contrast, are considered highly sensitive and complex technologies. Information about them is difficult to obtain and, again as Pakistan has discovered with its enrichment programme, certain crucial components like special steels and valves must be imported, at least initially.

LWRs, on the other hand, which depend on the slightly enriched uranium fuel cycle, are said to be cheaper to build but more expensive to operate. However, fuel-enrichment facilities are for the moment beyond the reach of all but the most industrially advanced countries. Such countries, moreover, are likely to impose their own political and economic conditions before they agree to export enriched fuel. The United States has retroactive legislation which stipulates that enriched uranium fuel can be exported only to countries that adhere to the Nuclear Non-Proliferation Treaty (NPT). This issue became a bone of contention between the United States and India, which has one LWR in service, built on a turn-key basis by General Electric in 1968, and which used to depend for its operations on enriched fuel from the United States.

Even countries that sign the NPT have no guarantee that they will be able to obtain the enriched fuel they require. Until a few years ago there was said to be a world-wide shortage of uranium and insufficient enrichment capacity to meet the needs of all LWRs. When Egypt signed a nuclear protocol with the United States in 1975 in order to import power reactors, it also had to agree to pay in advance for enrichment services that would not be required until at least a decade later.

In choosing between different fuel cycles and reactor systems, several political and economic variables have to be taken into account. For a developing country that seeks to preserve some independence of action in the future, one solution may be to opt for a mix of the natural-uranium and enriched-uranium fuel cycles to sustain both PHWRs and LWRs. For such a mixed choice, costs are bound to be higher than would be the case if a single common fuel cycle strategy were adopted. In the final analysis, choosing the most appropriate fuel cycle cannot be an easy decision.

NOTES

1. Sir John Cockroft, 'The future of atomic energy', *Bulletin of Atomic Scientists*, vol. 6, no. 11 (November 1950), pp. 235–329.

2. Arthur Holly Compton, *Atomic quest* (Oxford University Press, Oxford, 1956), p. 12.

3. *Nuclear energy and nuclear weapons proliferation* (SIPRI, Taylor and Francis, London, 1979), p. 390.

4. S.E. Hunt, *Fission, fusion and the energy crisis* (Pergamon, 1974), p. 28.

5. The *Observer* (London), 16 December 1979.

6. Ralph Nader and John Abbots, *The menace of atomic energy* (W.W. Norton, New York, 1977), pp. 25–55.

7. J. Rotblat, 'Nuclear energy and nuclear weapons proliferation', cited in *Nuclear energy and nuclear weapons proliferation*, p. 393.

8. Ibid, p. 410.

3

Israel

Israel is the first nuclear power of the Middle East. It has the longest-established programme of nuclear research in the region, the largest unsafeguarded reactor, the only confirmed and functioning plutonium-reprocessing plant and probably the biggest and best-qualified pool of scientists.

Although there is no proof that the country's scientists have ever carried out a nuclear test, all the available evidence, including the testimony of a disgruntled nuclear technician, Mordechai Vanunu, points to a formidable array of both fission and fusion devices. No Arab state can match this sophisticated capability and in the region only one other country, Pakistan, has successfully developed a nuclear weapons option. In 1974 a terse internal memorandum of the US Central Intelligence Agency (CIA) stated that Israel had acquired nuclear weapons:

> We believe that Israel already has produced nuclear weapons. Our judgement is based on Israeli acquisition of large quantities of uranium, partly by clandestine means; the ambiguous nature of Israeli efforts in the field of uranium enrichment; and Israel's large investment in a costly missile system designed to accommodate nuclear warheads.[1]

This was not the first assertion by Western intelligence analysts that Israel had crossed the nuclear threshold, but it was authoritative. The issue that the CIA assessment left unsolved was how the Israelis did it. The answer was provided twelve years later when a Moroccan Jew settled in Israel, resentful of the discrimination that he had experienced in the promised land, decided to tell his story. Mordechai Vanunu, who had previously worked at the Israeli nuclear research centre at Dimona, sold his story to the London-based *Sunday Times* before he was lured back to Israel to stand trial for his action.[2] The significance of Vanunu's revelation was his disclosure that Israel had a secret plutonium-reprocessing plant, built underground, at the Dimona nuclear research centre. It was long assumed that Israel had mastered reprocessing, at least at laboratory-scale level, but until Vanunu this was never confirmed.

The reprocessing plant was built with French help. After Vanunu's revelations appeared in the *Sunday Times*, Professor Francis Perrin, France's High Commissioner for Atomic Energy from 1951 to 1970, told the newspaper that as part of a 1957 agreement, the French government contracted to build both the Dimona reactor and a reprocessing plant.[3] Vanunu worked at a building called Machon 2, which was ostensibly a little-used warehouse, but actually disguised the existence of six underground floors where plutonium was reprocessed and later machined into components for nuclear weapons. His reference to 140 fuel rods from the Dimona reactor suggested that it had been upgraded from its original 26 MW to 150 MW, another tribute to the engineering skills of the Israelis. From used fuel rods of the reactor the Israelis have been able to extract up to 40 kilograms of plutonium per year.

Vanunu also revealed the existence of facilities for producing lithium 6, tritium and deuterium, which gives Israel the potential to build thermonuclear weapons. At the very least the production of lithium, tritium and deuterium showed that the Israelis had the raw materials to boost the yield of simple nuclear weapons by a factor of ten. Vanunu secretly used a camera to take more than 60 photographs of the interior of Machon 2. These photographs included models of fission bombs that were put on display for visiting Israeli VIPs.

British and American experts who debriefed Vanunu are convinced that Israel is an established nuclear weapons power and probably ranks sixth in the world after the United States, the Soviet Union, China, France and Britain. Dr Theodore Taylor, a former nuclear weapons consultant, told the *Sunday Times*: 'There should no longer be any doubt that Israel is, and for at least a decade has been, a fully fledged nuclear weapons state.' Dr Frank Barnaby, the distinguished British nuclear physicist and former director of the Stockholm International Peace Research Institute, said, 'I think it's conclusive. The photographs were further proof of what Vanunu was saying — that Israel has between 100 and 200 nuclear weapons and many could be thermonuclear.'[4]

Although Vanunu was best informed about the reprocessing technology at Machon 2, he also said Israeli scientists were experimenting with uranium enrichment by using centrifuges and lasers. Such experiments would not be surprising and would be in line with the Israeli determination to keep up with new developments in nuclear research. At one time the CIA actually suspected that Israeli scientists had made a breakthrough in laser enrichment, which meant their weapons were based on highly enriched uranium, but this theory was later discounted.

The Vanunu affair followed an investigative report in another British Sunday newspaper, the *Observer*, that Israel, helped by financial backing from the Shah of Iran, had developed a missile capable of carrying nuclear warheads.[5] The *Observer* report was based on secret documents taken by Iranian students from the Israeli trade mission in Tehran. They proved that as long ago as 1977 the Israelis tested the prototype of an improved Jericho-type missile capable of carrying a 750-kilogram warhead for up to 200 kilometres.

In 1977, when Israeli Foreign Minister Moshe Dayan discussed the missile project, code-named Operation Flower, with a visiting Iranian official, he said, 'The ground-to-ground missile can be regarded as a missile with a nuclear head'. The success of Operation Flower means Israel now also has a missile-based delivery system for its nuclear warheads. The combination of nuclear bombs and a proven missile-based delivery system makes Israel a formidable regional power.

THE ATOMIC ENERGY COMMISION (AEC)

The remarkable history of Israel's nuclear programme is almost as old as the state itself. It began in 1949 at the privately run Weizmann Institute near Tel Aviv with the founding of a string of high-powered nuclear research laboratories. They were for isotopes research, nuclear physics and physical chemistry, which dealt with theoretical physics, experimental physics and nuclear instrumentation.[6]

The AEC was established in 1952 by David Ben Gurion, the founding father of Israel and the country's first Prime Minister. The AEC's objectives, as outlined in 1952, were to advise the government on long-term policy issues, supervise the implementation of agreed policies, and to maintain contact with foreign scientific institutions.[7] It has not been widely understood that the AEC was affiliated from the outset to the Defence Ministry. In 1948 the Defence Ministry had organised geological surveys of the Negev to search for uranium, and in 1952 the new AEC was placed under the direct control and supervision of the Defence Ministry.[8]

Some Arab experts have claimed that Israel was able to build up its nuclear expertise with the active assistance of a talented pool of Jewish nuclear scientists from Europe, whose efforts contributed so much to the success of the Manhattan Project in the United States. In reality, the Israelis were only too aware of the importance of trained manpower and built up their own reservoir of scientists who, while they may have been trained abroad, had their feet very firmly planted in Israel. They included men like the physicist Yuval Neeman, who was born in Tel Aviv in 1925 and trained in Haifa and London. He became professor of physics at Tel Aviv University in 1965 and played an important role in the AEC.

The chemist Israel Dostrovsky was born in 1918 in Odessa and educated at London University. For a few years between 1942 and 1948 he was a lecturer at the University of Wales before he emigrated to Israel. It was Dostrovsky's discovery of a new way of producing heavy water, deuterium oxide, that was later bartered to the French. One of the most outstanding scientists was another chemist, the late Ernst Bergmann, who was born in Germany in 1904 and was a chemistry lecturer at Berlin University at the age of 16. Bergmann was scientific adviser to the Haganah in 1936 and later, after independence, became professor of organic chemistry at the Hebrew University. He was closely involved with the AEC and became chairman until he resigned in 1966 because of policy differences with Prime Minister Levi Eshkol. Bergmann's contribution to the work of the AEC was to help set up the reprocessing plant that was secretly obtained from the French in 1960. In 1966 he was awarded Israel's State Security Prize.

Israel's earliest foreign contacts in nuclear research were with the United States and France. In 1955, under President Eisenhower's Atoms for Peace proposals, the Americans agreed to build a 5 MW reactor at Nahal Soreq, and between 1955 and 1960 some 56 Israelis were trained at US Atomic Energy Commission centres at Argonne and Oak Ridge.[9] Far more important, as we shall see, was the agreement with France, which led to the construction of the nuclear research centre at Dimona. The relationship with France had its drawbacks. In 1957 the decision secretly to acquire a reactor, and presumably a reprocessing plant as well, led to the resignation of six out of seven AEC members. The sole exception was Bergmann.

The next major expansion took place in 1966, when the AEC was transferred from the Defence Ministry to the Prime Minister's office with an expanded membership of 20. The AEC's supervisory functions now extended over three divisions. These were licensing (regulatory licensing of all nuclear activities in the country), power and water (medium- and long-range planning of nuclear power in Israel) in single- and dual-purpose power plants and radiation and radio-isotope applications.[10]

DIMONA: CO-OPERATION WITH FRANCE

Soon after the AEC was established, France became the first Western power to show interest in Israel's technical expertise for heavy-water production, as well as uranium extraction. It may seem a little odd for France to seek co-operation with Israel in the nuclear field, given the vast difference in the size and resources of the two countries. However, in those years France was still an aspiring nuclear power, and one that was deliberately isolated from the nuclear research and development efforts of its wartime allies, the United States and Britain.

Although individual French scientists played an important role in wartime nuclear research, neither the Resistance nor the government in exile had the resources to promote nuclear research efforts that could match those of Germany, Britain or America. After the war had ended, the provisions of the McMahon Act in the United States excluded the French from sharing in the fruits of American nuclear activities. The British also went their own way, and although there were relations with Moscow, there was little prospect of the Soviets extending a helping hand to France. It was in this context that nuclear collaboration with Israel began. Even such collaboration might not have extended beyond a preliminary stage but for political developments that reinforced existing ties. Firstly, the 1956 Suez campaign, and later Nasser's support of the Algerian nationalists, had the effect of boosting links between Paris and Tel Aviv. It was only after General de Gaulle returned to power in France in 1958, followed by the subsequent promise of independence for Algeria, that the French started to review their links.

The 1953 protocol and nuclear co-operation agreement led to France's purchasing the patent for heavy-water production, which Dostrovsky invented, while in return Israel was given access to French nuclear facilities, where Israeli students were accepted for training.[11] Continued diplomatic and political co-operation paved the way for a new agreement in 1957, this time for constructing the secret nuclear plants at Dimona. Details of the agreement are still secret, and it was assumed they concerned only the construction of a reactor.[12] Since Vanunu's disclosures it has also become evident that the agreement also included a contract to build an underground nuclear-reprocessing plant. After Vanunu's story was published in 1986, former French Atomic Energy High Commissioner Professor Perrin admitted, 'In 1957 we agreed to build a reactor and a chemical plant for the production of plutonium.'

Although nuclear co-operation between France and Israel began to taper off in 1959, Perrin said that de Gaulle did not stop the construction of the reprocessing plant: 'We thought it would be good for France to have this possibility of working with Israel.'[13]

The French-Israeli agreement on nuclear co-operation has been the subject of speculation ever since it was signed in 1957. In 1981 authors Weissman and Krosney rightly concluded that the agreement was more far-reaching than had been suspected. They suggested it included a provision for spent fuel from Dimona to be reprocessed in France, which would then send the plutonium back to Israel.[14] In fact, as we now know, French willingness to build a reprocessing plant within Israel meant that there was no need to take back spent fuel from Dimona. The other part of the agreement, to build a reactor, was also meant to remain a secret, but in 1960 an American US spy plane spotted the site and the Israelis were forced to admit the truth. Ben Gurion, who had earlier described the construction in the desert as a textile factory, told the Knesset that the reactor would be used for peaceful scientific, medical and industrial purposes and would train scientists for future nuclear power stations.

Neither the reactor nor its fuel elements were subject to safeguards. This was still the pre-safeguards period, and France did not require nor Israel offer any safeguards commitment. Moreover, if the 1957 agreement also included the sharing of nuclear weapons testing data, as Weissman and Krosney have suggested, a safeguards agreement would have been irrelevant.[15] Subsequent attempts by the French to impose conditions on the sale of nuclear fuel to Israel would have come too late. The development of a fuel-fabrication facility has been well within Israel's scientific capabilities, and for uranium ore there were a number of sources to choose from.

NAHAL SOREQ: CO-OPERATION WITH THE UNITED STATES

Throughout the course of their nuclear research the Israelis have always sought to maintain close relations with the United States, although Washington was prepared only to provide limited help. This began in July 1955 after an agreement was signed to give Israel a small 1 MW research reactor, as well as a library of books on nuclear research.[16] The initial fuel charge of the reactor was 6 kilograms of uranium that had been enriched to 20 per cent. The background to this transfer of technology was President Eisenhower's 1953 Atoms for Peace proposals, as well as the Atomic Energy Act of 1954, which permitted the export of experimental reactors and the release of previously restricted data on nuclear subjects.

In 1958 Israel renegotiated the 1955 agreement to upgrade the reactor, which was at Nahal Soreq, and run it on 90 per cent enriched fuel. In view of these changes Washington insisted on a system of bilateral inspection and safeguards measures for Nahal Soreq. It also obtained a commitment by Israel to return the enriched fuel elements after they had been fully utilised.[17]

In 1965, after a trilateral agreement between the United States, Israel and the IAEA, the safeguards and inspection procedures were transferred to the IAEA. Nahal Soreq, code-named IRR 1, conducts research in nuclear physics, chemistry and biochemistry. Unlike Dimona, it has been open to foreign students and provides Israelis with an opportunity of keeping in touch with the international scientific community.

Relations with Washington were strained almost to breaking point in 1960 when the US spy plane spotted the tell-tale dome of the Dimona reactor. There was consternation in Washington, followed by threats to cut off all nuclear assistance to Israel. Eventually, after considerable pressure from President Kennedy, Israel was forced to agree to American inspection visits. These were clearly less than full-scale inspections and provided only tentative confirmation that Dimona was being used exclusively for peaceful purposes. However, in 1969 a team of inspectors reportedly submitted a written complaint that they could not guarantee that there was no weapons-related work at Dimona, in view of the hurried and limited nature of the inspection permitted by the Israeli authorities.[18]

The secrecy and security that have always surrounded Dimona were reflected in a *Der Spiegel* report of 1969, which claimed that an Israeli fighter plane was shot down and its pilot killed when it strayed by accident into the area during the 1967 War. To avoid legitimising any clandestine weapons research that could have been going on at Dimona, in 1969 the United States stopped all further inspection visits to the site; but efforts continued to persuade Israel to sign the NPT.

DIMONA FUEL

France provided the initial fuel requirements of the Dimona reactor, which to begin with were estimated at 24 tons of natural uranium per year. This was based on the assumption that Dimona was a 24 MW reactor. However, after the reactor was upgraded, probably after the 1967 Middle East War, there would have been a steep increase in the quantities of uranium needed for the reactor.

Where did Israel get its uranium from? Some would have been mined in the Negev, possibly as a by-product of the phosphate industry; and South Africa, in the light of the friendly relations that later developed with Pretoria, was almost certainly another source. Another intriguing possibility was suggested by the American magazine *Rolling Stone*, which claimed that a special Israeli commando squad had been set up to hijack lorry-loads of uranium ore from France and Britain.[19] It was the Israelis again, according to this theory, who were responsible for hijacking 200 tons of low-grade uranium ore from a rusty German freighter — the Scheersberg A — as it made its way from Genoa to Antwerp in November 1968.

ENRICHED URANIUM

The theft of uranium ore is quite separate from another well-documented incident involving the disappearance of highly enriched or weapons-grade uranium from the United States. We know from earlier CIA suspicions that Israeli scientists have been experimenting with new methods of enriching uranium, and Vanunu has confirmed that research is being conducted in both laser and centrifuge enrichment technology.

In 1968 the United States AEC discovered that at least 200 tons of highly enriched uranium had gone missing from a fuel-fabrication plant, the Nuclear Materials and Equipment Corporation (NUMEC), in Apollo, Pennsylvania. The CIA first suspected the uranium had gone to China, but then the finger pointed to the president of NUMEC, Mr Zalman Shapiro, who had close ties with Israel. Shapiro was fined for the missing uranium, although he always denied the charge that he had sent the material to Israel. Former CIA officials, however, continue to believe that the missing uranium of weapons-grade quality was diverted to Israel.[20]

THE SEARCH FOR NUCLEAR POWER PLANTS

Although Israeli nuclear research has been heavily influenced by military considerations, political leaders have from time to time expressed interest in the civil uses of nuclear power. The absence of any significant oil reserves, and the shortage of water, gave the Israelis a legitimate interest in acquiring nuclear power and desalination plants. From 1962 the Israeli government was in the market for a dual-purpose nuclear power plant that would generate electric power and desalinate water.

In 1965 Israeli Prime Minister Eshkol negotiated an agreement with the United States for an engineering and economic feasibility study to build a dual-purpose nuclear power plant. The study, concluded in 1966, argued that a dual-purpose plant for generating 200 MW of electricity, and desalinating 100 million gallons of water per day, was economically feasible.[21] The plant was scheduled to start operating by 1972 at Nizanim, north of Ashkelon, but the project led to bitter controversy in Israel. Doubts were expressed about the economic competitiveness of nuclear desalination, and there was concern at the safeguards that the United States might seek to impose. There was also the question of raising the $200 million that the plant was expected to cost. The project was revived in 1974 with President Nixon's offer to supply American nuclear power reactors to both Egypt and Israel, but it was not followed up.

In 1976 the Israeli government signed a letter of intent to purchase two LWRs from the United States, with the first reactor to be built at Nizanim. This attempt at investing in nuclear civil power fell foul of the Carter Administration's nuclear policy review and the NNPA of 1978. The terms of the Act required nuclear-buying countries to accept comprehensive safeguards in exchange for US nuclear technology. Such a condition, which would have meant opening up Dimona to foreign inspectors, was unacceptable to Israel.

GOVERNMENT ATTITUDES TO WEAPONS

Despite the overwhelming evidence provided by Vanunu, the Israelis refuse to admit they have an arsenal of sophisticated nuclear weapons. The official response to questions arising from Vanunu's disclosures was to repeat the old statement that Israel would not be the first to introduce nuclear weapons into the Middle East.[22]

Since NATO and Warsaw Pact warships equipped with nuclear

weapons have cruised in the Mediterranean for years, this gives the Israelis a let-out clause if they should decide in the future to make their weapons capability explicit. The country's political leaders have hinted at Israel's nuclear potential, but they have stopped short of admitting anything substantial. In 1968 Prime Minister Eshkol said that Israel had the technical knowledge to make nuclear weapons, but a significant gap existed between the technological knowledge and its application in weapons design.[23] The nearest the Israelis have come to admitting anything substantial was a 1974 statement by President Ephraim Katzir, in which he told a group of science writers that it had always been the intention to provide the potential for nuclear development. 'We now have that potential', he told them. 'We will defend this country with all possible means at hand. We have to develop more powerful and new arms to protect ourselves.'[24]

The earliest intelligence reports stating that Israel had acquired nuclear weapons date back to 1968. According to one account, this was based on Israeli jet fighters practising manoeuvres that only made sense as part of a nuclear-bomb-carrying strategy. Another account has CIA director Richard Helms warning President Johnson that Israel had nuclear weapons. According to this version, Johnson ordered Helms not to tell anyone else.[25] The 1974 CIA internal memorandum, noted earlier in this chapter, was by far the most authoritative source and left no room for doubt that Israel had crossed the nuclear threshold and was rapidly building up a nuclear arsenal. It was this assessment that led *Time* magazine to conclude two years later that Israel had stockpiled 13 nuclear bombs.

The last serious attempt at assessing the Israeli nuclear stockpile — until Vanunu appeared — was by the Georgetown University Institute of Strategic Studies in the United States. This report claimed that Israel had between 50 and 100 nuclear bombs and would have built up a reserve of 100 nuclear bombs by the end of the century.[26] Analysts from the Institute correctly pinpointed Dimona as the country's nuclear material-producing centre (plutonium) and suggested that production capacity had trebled. Such an estimate, post-Vanunu, now seems conservative.

Current Israeli policy is still based on a strategy of calculated ambiguity that aims to project strength based on a *possible* weapons capability. By not admitting to their nuclear weapons, the Israelis avoid sanctions from allies like the United States. They also deny their Arab enemies an incentive to take up the nuclear challenge. How long such a strategy can be sustained is another issue.

Not all Israelis believe in the doctrine of nuclear ambiguity. Shai

Feldman, of Tel Aviv University's Centre for Strategic Studies, has argued that nuclear weapons have a deterrence value and should be part of an explicit strategic doctrine. 'By providing effective deterrence, nuclear weapons have the capacity to reduce the likelihood of war, both conventional and nuclear', Feldman argued in a book published in 1982.[27] An explicit nuclear posture would also deter enemies from lower levels of violence such as guerrilla warfare and wars of attrition. The Feldman thesis, qualified by proposals for political flexibility in other areas, may still be too radical for the country's leaders, but some Israelis have clearly started questioning the old policy of ambiguity.

'Can Israel continue to use a three-decades-old formula in the post-Vanunu era?', asked Hirsh Goodman, the respected military correspondent of the *Jerusalem Post*. He continued:[28]

> Israel's official position has been and remains that it will not be the first country to introduce nuclear weapons in the region. The advent of Vanunu, however, coupled with Israel's official reaction to his alleged perfidy, places this attitude in question . . .
>
> The old formulations used to obfuscate . . . the subject have, to all intents and purposes, lost their relevance. A new level of discussion becomes unavoidable.

TESTING THE WEAPONS

Does Israel need to test its nuclear weapons? Arab leaders, while conceding Jerusalem's technological advances in the nuclear field, have pointed out that there is no evidence that any weapons have been tested. The issue will be raised again and again as other countries approach the threshold that Israel has crossed. It is an issue that has been actively considered, for example, in Pakistan, where scientists say they can simulate nuclear tests with the help of computers.

Most experts agree that testing is not vital for simple Nagasaki-type bombs. Even if Israel had access to French test data earlier, the need to test becomes more pressing as weapons become more sophisticated and cross into the thermonuclear range. Vanunu's evidence points to Israeli scientists experimenting with thermonuclear bombs, which raises the question of how and when they may have been tested. Rumours have been circulating since 1963 that the Israelis have tested at least one nuclear weapon. In 1963 a West German magazine claimed that a small underground test had been conducted in the Negev,[29] but this was almost certainly untrue since the Dimona reactor and reprocessing plant were barely operational and the Israelis had no access to weapons-grade material of their own.

Far more significant is the strategic co-operation between Israel and South Africa, which many believe led to the joint testing of a nuclear bomb in the southern Atlantic. Black African leaders have been worried by evidence of high-level exchanges of scientific and military intelligence between Israel and South Africa. Especially significant was the November 1979 visit to South Africa by Major-General Amos Horev, former chief scientist of the Israeli Defence Ministry, who later took up the job of president of Technion. The Israeli Defence Ministry maintains direct links with Technion.

In South Africa Horev's programme included visits to the national atomic research centre in Pelindaba, the nuclear centre in Valindaba, the nuclear complex at Koeberg and the naval base at Simonstown.[30] The Horev visit took place in the wake of the controversial double flash of light, characteristic of a nuclear bomb explosion, recorded by an American Vela satellite.[31] Although an *ad hoc* panel of non-governmental scientists brought together by President Carter could not agree on the meaning of the double flash, intelligence sources believe it was the signature of a nuclear test jointly carried out by Israel and South Africa. Those who disagreed with this assessment did not realise the advanced stage that Israel, and to a lesser extent South Africa, had reached with their nuclear weapons research. In the light of what Vanunu brought out of Israel, this might be an opportune time to re-examine the data of the Vela satellite.

Israel's nuclear progress was bound to affect her Arab neighbours. For all their dislike of the Zionist state, the Arabs could not afford to ignore the strategic implications of Israel's nuclear interests. Succeeding chapters, starting with Egypt, chart Arab reactions and the efforts that were made to keep up with Israel.

NOTES

1. US Government, *Prospects for further proliferation of nuclear weapons*, DCI N10 1945/74, 4 September 1974.
2. The *Sunday Times*, 5 October 1986.
3. The *Sunday Times*, 12 October, 1986.
4. Interview with the author, April 1987.
5. The *Observer*, 2 February 1986.
6. Meyer Weisgal and Joel Carmichael, *Chaim Weizmann: a biography by several hands* (Weidenfeld and Nicolson, London, 1962).

7. Fuad Jabber, *Israel and nuclear weapons* (Chatto and Windus, London, 1971), p. 18.

8. Peter Pry, *Israel's nuclear arsenal* (Croom Helm, London, 1984).

9. Ibid.

10. *Scientific Research in Israel* (Israel Council for Research and Development, Jerusalem, 1976), p. 216.

11. Michael Bar Zohar, *Suez ultra-secret* (Fayard, Paris, 1964), p. 62.

12. Leonard Beaton and John Maddox, *The spread of nuclear weapons* (Chatto and Windus, London, 1962), p. 172.

13. Perrin, the *Sunday Times*.

14. Steve Weissman and Herbert Krosney, *The Islamic bomb* (Times Books, New York, 1981), p. 118.

15. Weissman and Krosney, *The Islamic bomb*, p. 114.

16. *US treaties and other international agreements*, vol. 6, part. 2, pp. 2642-6, cited in the *New York Times*, 9 September 1955.

17. US Congress Joint Committee on Atomic Energy, *Background material for the review of the international atomic policies and programs of the US*, vol. 3 (GPO, Washington, D.C., 1960), p. 853.

18. *New York Times*, 18 July 1970.

19. *Rolling Stone*, 1 December 1977.

20. Weissman and Krosney, *The Islamic bomb*, p. 124.

21. *Economic feasibility and economic study for dual-purpose electric desalinating plant for Israel* (Kaiser Engineering, California, January 1966).

22. The *Guardian*, 17 November 1986.

23. *World armaments and disarmament* (SIPRI Yearbook, Stockholm, 1972).

24. Brian Beckett, *Israel's nuclear options* (Middle East International, London, November 1976).

25. Peter Pry, *Israel's nuclear arsenal*, p. 40.

26. *Jane's Defence Weekly*, 15 December 1984.

27. Shai Feldman, *Israeli nuclear deterrence* (Columbia University Press, New York, 1982), pp. 240-3.

28. *Jerusalem Post*, 5 December 1986.

29. Zdenek Cervenka and Barbara Rogers, *The nuclear axis* (Times Books, New York, 1978), p. 318.

30. *Rand Daily Mail*, 8 November 1979.

31. *Rand Daily Mail*, 3 February 1980.

4

Egypt

Israel's nuclear research was of immediate concern to her most powerful neighbour, Egypt, which warned of retaliation if Israel went ahead with developing nuclear weapons. Yet despite such warnings, particularly from President Nasser, the Egyptian nuclear effort remained pitiful in comparison with that of Israel. Nasser's scientists seemed to lack the consistent political backing that their counterparts enjoyed in Israel.

It may be that Nasser had faith, perhaps too much faith, in the conventional superiority of Arab armies, or possibly he thought that Cairo's traditional ally, the Soviet Union, would provide nuclear weapons on request. This never happened, however, and when the Egyptians did try to secure nuclear weapons from the Chinese, they were turned down. By that time, after 1967, the Israelis had a well-established nuclear superiority, although the Egyptians never quite knew what precisely had been achieved at Dimona. There were sporadic efforts to build up a nuclear infrastructure in Egypt, but such efforts came too late and never achieved fruition. The Egyptian government's greatest success in nuclear matters, which remains true today, has been that of training large numbers of competent scientists.

This chapter examines Egyptian reactions to Israel's progress in nuclear research, before discussing Cairo's relatively late entry into the nuclear age and some of the individuals associated with the founding of the Atomic Energy Establishment (AEE). It goes on to discuss the structure of the AEE and some of the directors who have been in charge of it. The chapter also discusses the AEE's repeated attempts since 1957 to expand nuclear research, particularly in the light of Israel's progress. Egypt's efforts since 1964 to harness nuclear energy for electric power production are also surveyed in some detail.

REACTIONS TO ISRAEL

The disclosure of the Dimona reactor, followed by reports that Israel was making nuclear weapons, brought a sharp response from President Nasser of Egypt, who warned in 1961 that the Arabs would wage a preventative war, 'even if we have to mobilise four million people'. If Israel were given nuclear weapons, 'We will secure atomic weapons at any cost.'[1]

These warnings that Egypt would be bound to retaliate if Israel acquired nuclear arms were repeated at regular intervals by Nasser's aides. They show that the Egyptians were suspicious of Israel, but ignorant of what had been achieved. Right up to 1980 and beyond, when the Sadat Government conceded that Israel had the technological capability to make weapons, there was some doubt whether Tel Aviv had taken the final step and crossed the nuclear threshold by making weapons. In 1980 Foreign Minister Kamal Hasan Ali told the People's Assembly in Cairo:[2] 'Since the 1960s Israel has had the capability to produce nuclear weapons in the Dimona reactor. However, there is no evidence that Israel has actually produced such weapons, or that it has conducted a nuclear test.'

Nasser's earlier concern with Dimona encouraged Egyptian scientists to pursue their own research vigorously, but Nasser never seems to have considered the possibility of backing a crash programme of nuclear development. He was at least as interested in building up the country's conventional defence. Nuclear research did not have the same priority as, for instance, his well-documented efforts to use German expertise for building rockets capable of hitting Israeli targets.[3] Later, more urgent, efforts at expanding the country's nuclear research facilities, when Israel already had a plutonium-producing reactor and a functioning reprocessing plant, came too late and were hampered by the effects of two Middle East wars.

ORIGINS

Egypt was in any case a late starter in the nuclear field. Unlike Israel the Egyptian Board of Atomic Energy was not created until 1955. Its functions were to formulate policy for an Atomic Energy Establishment (AEE) that would in turn conduct research into the peaceful uses of nuclear energy. This delay in setting up a nuclear research organisation in Egypt was the result of political uncertainties after the Second World War, which prevented the formulation of any coherent policy.

The weaknesses of successive governments, that rose and fell at the behest of the King or the British authorities, the Palestine War of 1948 and, finally, the instability caused by the 1952 revolution, all contributed to the absence of a coherent national policy. On the other hand, the education of scientists at home and abroad was not interrupted. By 1952, the year of the revolution, the number of Egyptian science graduates was estimated at just under 1,400,[4] slightly more than has been assessed for China in the same year.

Out of these 1,400 graduates, including holders of PhD degrees, the vast majority specialised in medicine, followed by agriculture, engineering and chemistry. A nuclear programme established then would have been able to draw upon an already existing pool of scientists from many different disciplines. By 1952 some scientists from within this pool were already expressing an interest in nuclear research in so far as it affected their field of specialisation. Medical doctors, for instance, wanted to use radioactive isotopes in their hospitals and a school of physicists at Cairo University wanted to acquire a Vandergraaf accelerator to study charged particles.[5] State backing for such groups, however, was still a few years away.

EARLY STIRRINGS

The founding of the Board of Atomic Energy, and also the AEE, in 1955 coincided with the establishment of a stable government under Gamal Abdel Nasser, who had masterminded the overthrow of King Farouk three years earlier in 1952. However, calmer political waters constituted only one factor that contributed to the formulation of a national nuclear policy. As we have seen, individual scientists, whether doctors or physicists, had already expressed an interest in nuclear research. Also important in formulating policy was the experience gained by individuals who had worked in the laboratories of research institutes in Western countries. A third contributory factor was the impact on Egyptian scientists of the first Conference on the Peaceful Uses of Atomic Energy, held in Geneva in 1955.

The Egyptian delegation to this conference consisted of Dr Ahmed Riad Turki, a professor of chemistry at Cairo University; Dr Mustapha Nazif, president of Ain Shams University and Dean of the Faculty of Engineering at Cairo University; Dr Ibrahim Hilmy Abdel Rahman, an English-trained astronomer of the University of London, who had recently returned to Egypt; and Professor El Halawani, an Egyptian health specialist, who was Under-Secretary to the Ministry of Family Planning. During their stay in Geneva the delegation made contact with two young researchers who were completing their doctoral dissertations in Paris. They were Abdel Maaboud El Guibaily, who was writing a thesis on nuclear chemistry at the Curie Laboratory; and Ismail Hazza, who had specialised in cosmic ray physics. Both men later returned to Egypt after obtaining their degrees. Hazza was later to play a leading role in setting up isotope laboratories in Egypt. El Guibaily, after serving as the head of nuclear chemistry at the AEE Research Centre in Inchas, went on to become Director-General of the AEE and Minister of Scientific Research. He retired from the government in 1976.

At Geneva the delegation had more of a watching brief, since nuclear science was still a new subject for Egyptians and few papers had been prepared for presentation to the conference. The only scientific paper from the Egyptians was prepared by Professor Riad Turki. It was on the subject of uranyl strychnine fluoride and it was based on a doctoral dissertation prepared by one of his former students.

LAYING THE FOUNDATIONS OF THE AEE

Back home in Egypt the year 1955 was also a hectic time for activity in the nuclear field. In March 1955 the government convened a committee of scientists and Free Officers to discuss what could be done to promote nuclear research. Based on the committee's recommendations a Board of Atomic Energy was created to supervise the activities of an AEE. The Board's duties were listed as promoting the peaceful uses of atomic energy by, in the first instance, training scientists in the relevant nuclear disciplines.

The principal departments that had already been formed, or else were in the process of being expanded, totalled eight. Collectively they comprised the nucleus of the AEE: mathematics and theoretical physics, experimental nuclear physics, nuclear chemistry, geology and raw materials, radio isotopes and their applications, radiation protection and civil defence, engineering and scientific equipment and reactors. Between 1955 and 1957 the Board encouraged the development of research groups within these departments. Missions were also sent abroad to study the organisation of nuclear research in other countries. The countries they visited in this period included the United States, Britain, France, the Soviet Union, West Germany, India, Austria, Denmark, Sweden and Holland.

A key figure in both the Board and the AEE was the astronomer

Ibrahim Hilmy Abdel Rahman. He has been described by his former colleagues as something of a science all-rounder, and when he returned home from England in 1954 he was fortunate to enjoy the confidence of Nasser, who appointed him Secretary-General to the then Council of Ministers. Besides his formal governmental duties, Abdel Rahman was responsible for establishing the first Egyptian Planning Institute and the Council for Scientific Research, the predecessor of the present-day Academy of Science. When the Board of Atomic Energy was founded in 1955, he was appointed its first Secretary-General. The chairman of the board was a former Free officer, Mr Kamal El Din Hussein, who was also to become Minister of Education.

Abdel Rahman also negotiated the first nuclear protocol with the Soviet Union in 1957. Relations between Cairo and Moscow had been steadily improving since 1955, when the Soviets supplied Egypt with light arms through Czechoslovakia. There was a further improvement after the 1956 Suez campaign when Khrushchev threatened retaliation against Britain and France if they did not withdraw their forces from Egypt. In the honeymoon period that followed Suez, the Soviet Union gave Egypt military and economic aid, which included equipping the National Nuclear Research Centre at Inchas.

Under the terms of the protocol the Soviet Union agreed to supply a small experimental reactor for Inchas, 40 kilometres north-east of Cairo, as well as the equipment for a theoretical physics laboratory. The latter included a Vandergraaf 2.5 MW accelerator, which Egyptian scientists had been interested in since 1954. Abdel Rahman also persuaded the Soviet authorities to accept Egypt's most promising secondary-school science graduates for further training.

THE CONSTRUCTION OF INCHAS

By 1957 the Board of Atomic Energy had selected a site for the country's first nuclear research centre. They chose a four-square-mile plot of desert land that was remote enough to be considered safe for both health and security reasons. It was not far from the capital — only 40 kilometres — so scientists would not find it difficult to commute from their homes.

The physical security of the centre was an important early consideration. Since it was intended to handle radioactive material at the centre, measures had to be taken to prevent the infiltration of saboteurs. The remoteness of the site was ideal from this security standpoint. It was located in the Abu Zaabal region, where the government intended to set up a number of military factories. The entire area, Inchas included, was classified as a high-security area, heavily protected at all times by the army.

The Soviet proposal for Inchas was firstly to start up the reactor engineering department, for which they were supplying the small experimental reactor, followed by theoretical physics, health physics, chemistry, engineering and the others. Because of construction and delivery delays, however, the reactor did not go critical until July 1961 — two years later than scheduled. The first department to start functioning at the site was theoretical physics, for which the Soviet Union provided a Vandergraaf. This was followed by health physics, neutron physics and chemistry. Both neutron physics and theoretical physics came under the supervision of Professor Mohammed El Naadi, a London-trained theoretical physicist and former Vice-Chancellor of El Mansoura University, widely respected by his colleagues and today considered the father of modern physics-teaching in Egypt.

Chemistry, complete with a radio isotope laboratory, was in due course given into the joint charge of El Guibaily, who returned to Egypt in 1959 after spending a year at the Nuclear Institute in Norway. He ran the department together with another chemist, Dr Michel Farah, until he was promoted to the position of Director-General of the AEE in 1965. El Guibaily's friend and colleague in Paris, the late Ismail Hazza, preceded him to Cairo, where he started up isotope research centres. He was responsible for founding the regional centre for isotopes research in the Dokki district of Cairo.

CHANGES IN THE BOARD AND THE AEE FROM 1959

The Board of Atomic Energy became less active as Inchas began to take shape. Day-to-day management of the centre was given to the Director-General of Inchas. Logically, the job should have gone to Abdel Rahman, who had played such an important role in setting up the Board and the AEE; but his interests were elsewhere — for example, in working for the United Nations International Development Organisation — and the choice of the first Director-General for the AEE fell on Mr Salah Hedayat, a Free Officer and chemistry graduate, who helped to make bombs for Nasser before the revolution. Hedayat, who ran the AEE between 1959 and 1961 with the help of El Nadi, the physicist, represented the interests of the Defence Ministry. A former student of Riad Turki, he came to Nasser's notice in the late 1940s for his work in making guns and bombs for the

52

Palestinian War and also for use against the British and Wafdists in Egypt.

When Kamal El Din Hussein retired as chairman of the Atomic Energy Board in 1961, Hedayat succeeded him. Between 1961 and 1965 he was Chairman of the Board of Atomic Energy, Director-General of the AEE and Minister of Scientific Research. In 1965 he was succeeded as Chairman of the Board by Dr Hussein Sait, another Free Officer and Deputy Prime Minister. Sait was followed successively by two Ministers of Education, Dr Mohammed Azat Salama from 1967 to 1970, and Dr Ahmed Mustapha from 1970 to 1973.

The President of the National Academy of Science, Dr Abu El Azm, was Board Chairman from 1973 to 1976. From 1976 onwards the job of Chairman has once again been joined with that of the Director-General of the AEE. Dr Kamal Effat, a physicist, was Board Chairman and Director-General from 1976, and another physicist, Dr Ibrahim Hamouda, succeeded him in 1980. El Guibaily was Director-General of the AEE from 1965 until 1973, when he was appointed Minister of State for Scientific Research. He retired from public life in 1976.

MORE CHANGES AFTER 1976

In 1976, after President Nixon's visit to Cairo and his offer to provide two nuclear power plants to Egypt, a group of nuclear engineers was lured away from the AEE to constitute a new body, the Nuclear Power Plants Authority (NPPA). The first head of the NPPA was a civil engineer, Mr Hussein Sirry, directly answerable to the Ministry of Electricity. The new organisation was required to negotiate the purchase of nuclear power reactors and then run them once they were installed. For the next two years the AEE remained a semi-autonomous body under the Board of Atomic Energy and responsible via the Minister of Scientific Research to the President. In 1978, however, both the Board and the AEE were brought under the Ministry of Electricity.

One other change affected the AEE in this period. In 1977 the AEE's geology laboratories were hived off to form a separate unit, the Nuclear Materials Organisation, with Dr Mohammed El Shazly as the first Chairman. El Shazly was given more authority than he had previously enjoyed as the mere head of the geology section at Inchas. He was also given a separate budget and a new ministry, the Ministry of Trade, to which his organisation was attached.

THE IMPACT OF ISRAEL

In 1959 a young Egyptian physicist working at the Argonne nuclear research centre in the United States noticed two Israeli scientists at the same centre were researching the chemistry of plutonium-reprocessing. Alarmed by what he saw, he wrote home to the authorities, pointing out the significance of the Israelis' interest. The Egyptian physicist, Dr Eizzat Abdel Aziz, later to be appointed head of Inchas, never had any response to his letter. Perhaps a response was not necessary because, by 1960, when the existence of Dimona was revealed, it was self-evident that the Israelis were taking a serious interest in all aspects of nuclear research.

The clandestine manner in which the Dimona reactor was built inevitably fuelled suspicions about Israel's nuclear ambitions. The disclosure of Dimona may have spurred on the Egyptians to make a greater effort themselves. From 1960 onwards, probably as a response to Israel, there was a quickening of tempo in Egypt's nuclear programme. More students were encouraged to take an interest in the nuclear sciences, especially at postgraduate level.

The establishment of a nuclear engineering department at Alexandria University in 1962, the first department of its kind in the Arab world, was another step in the same direction. Money was made available from the government of Kuwait.[6] State scholarships were given to postgraduate students who managed to win a place at a reputable foreign university to study nuclear sciences. Other evidence of a quickening tempo was in the efforts to upgrade the Inchas reactor, or, failing that, to acquire a more powerful research reactor that would match what the Israelis were building at Dimona. The Inchas reactor went critical in 1961 and Soviet specialists who were consulted about upgrading it counselled patience. They said it was important to gain experience of running a small reactor before graduating to a bigger one.

Private Western companies were approached about selling a larger experimental reactor, or even a large power reactor, to Egypt.

During the third UN International Conference on the Peaceful Uses of Atomic Energy, El Guibaily and others spoke of plans for setting up a nuclear power reactor of 200 MW, far bigger than Dimona. The paper they presented said that the search for nuclear power was not inspired by any sense of economic urgency, nor did nuclear power stations of the projected size compete favourably with thermal stations:

The object of this project [was], in addition to the production of electricity, to introduce nuclear power technology and experience and to train personnel in the various disciplines required to face the needs of an expanding nuclear power programme starting from 1972.

El Guibaily's analysis was that existing thermal power plants would meet the country's needs until 1972. After that date, plans for increasing installed electrical generating capacity would depend partly on nuclear power. The paper's conclusions reflected the results of an energy survey jointly carried out the previous year — 1963 — by the AEE and the Ministry of Electricity. Following that, a panel of IAEA experts was invited to suggest future sites for nuclear power stations. The panel suggested Inchas, Burg El Arab, adjacant to a later preferred site at Sidi Kreir, west of Alexandria, and Wady Hof, south of Cairo. Two other sites were added later as future possibilities. They were Fayoum on Lake Quaroon, 80 kilometres south-west of Cairo, and El Tahrir, 60 kilometres north of Cairo. The master plan was to have at least one nuclear power station of 200 MW operating at one of these five sites by 1972. By the time the UN conference started, negotiations were already well advanced with a West German company, Siemens, to build a natural-uranium-fuelled heavy-water reactor (HWR) at Burg El Arab. Simultaneously, the authorities were studying the feasibility of building a heavy-water plant in Upper Egypt, near Aswan.

In 1964 the Soviet Union was asked to help set up a radio chemistry division, including 'hot labs', at Inchas, which would give Egyptian scientists laboratory-level experience of reprocessing and waste management for the nuclear waste that would be produced from the Siemens reactor. However, these ambitious plans for extending Inchas were suspended when the Siemens deal was cancelled by Egypt in 1965. This followed the rupture of diplomatic relations between Cairo and Bonn arising from the controversial sale of German tanks to Israel. Preliminary discussions were then held with three American companies, Westinghouse, General Electric and Combustion Engineering, but these contacts were suspended after the shock of defeat in the 1967 Middle East War.

Egypt's determination to catch up with Israel was strongest in the period up to 1967. Efforts were made to acquire a bigger reactor, together with supporting fuel-cycle facilities, but firstly the diplomatic break with Bonn, and then the 1967 War, which froze all AEE expenditure, put an end to all such plans. Furthermore, after 1967 the non-proliferation regime of the NPT imposed limitations on

Egypt's nuclear hopes. Egypt signed the NPT in 1970, but did not ratify it on the grounds that Israel had not done so. The effect of this refusal was to make it more difficult for supplier countries to sell anything but the most rudimentary elements of the fuel cycle to Cairo.

After 1967, according to Egyptian scientific sources, Egypt sought more help from friendly foreign governments to upgrade the country's nuclear facilities. After relying initially on the Soviet Union, Nasser turned to Peking for nuclear assistance. Just after the 1967 War, according to Egyptian sources, Nasser sent a delegation to Peking to ask if the Chinese would help Egypt upgrade its nuclear expertise. According to one Egyptian source, enquiries were made about purchasing nuclear weapons from Peking. The delegation was led by El Guibaily and included Effat as well as Professor Hasan El Mofty, then head of the reactors division at Inchas. The discussions were secret, but in response to questions about help in 'sensitive' areas of nuclear technology, the Chinese, who had carried out their first nuclear test in 1964, replied that in such matters self-help was the best solution. This reply was similar to the one given to Colonel Qadhafi of Libya a few years later when he sent a delegation to Peking with a similar appeal for expert assistance.

Although El Guibaily returned home empty-handed from Peking, prominent individuals tried their best to keep alive government interest in the country's nuclear programme. A critical role was played by Salah Hedayat, who had resigned from both the government and the AEE after a series of bitter arguments about the country's nuclear aims. Hedayat was especially critical about the lack of discipline at Inchas. He took personal credit for getting the experimental reactor commissioned, particularly since the Soviet government had threatened to withdraw from the project because of the inefficiency and endless delays its experts encountered.

Although he resigned from the Cabinet and the AEE, Hedayat kept up his links with the government by accepting the position of scientific adviser to Nasser from 1965 to 1970. In 1965 he also established under his chairmanship a nuclear engineering consultancy group, the Design Consultants Association (DCA), for which he obtained government funding. Members of the DCA were selected from Egyptian scientists working both at home and abroad. They were brought together ostensibly to provide consultancy services for a wide variety of engineering projects in the Arab world, but Hedayat saw the DCA's principal function as being one of helping Egypt to build an independent nuclear fuel cycle, based on a PHWR. By taking his expertise out of government, Hedayat thought he would be able to achieve his objectives more easily. He was backed in his plans by his friend and mentor, Nasser's Defence Minister, the late Abdel Hakim Amer. Like Hedayat, Amer was convinced that Israel was developing nuclear weapons and that something had to be done in Egypt to match the Israeli capacity.

In a series of detailed and confidential proposals made after 1965, the DCA proposed the building in Egypt of all the components of a nuclear fuel cycle, from a uranium-extracting plant near Inchas to a plutonium-yielding reactor and a reprocessing facility. To those of his critics who argued that the project would be prohibitively expensive, Hedayat replied that funding would be easy to obtain from brother Arab countries. The Kuwaitis had already come up with the funds for the nuclear engineering department at Alexandria and there were others, Hedayat believed, who would be just as willing.

A few years later Hedayat was appointed Minister of Science in the short-lived Federation Government of Egypt and Libya that was proclaimed in 1970. It was after his appointment as a minister in the Federation that he won Libyan President Muammar Qadhafi's support for a DCA-designed dual-purpose 40 MW nuclear desalination plant to be constructed in Alexandria. The plan was later shelved, first because of Nasser's death, and also because of strains in the relationship between Cairo and Tripoli. Libyan money for the DCA never materialised.

The DCA project nevertheless aroused tremendous jealousies within the AEE, and many of Hedayat's former colleagues were later to describe his proposals as eccentric and unworkable. Questions were subsequently raised about Hedayat's scientific capability since he was, as envious rivals pointed out, a mere honours graduate in chemistry. It would be a mistake, however, to undervalue what Hedayat proposed. If he had succeeded, Egypt would today have a nuclear infrastructure that would be more than a match for Israel's.

PLANNING FOR NUCLEAR POWER AFTER 1965

Hedayat's departure from the AEE coincided with a renewed drive for a nuclear power reactor. After the failure of the Siemens negotiations, the AEE turned to Westinghouse for a dual-purpose nuclear power station and desalination plant at Burg El Arab. A letter of intent was signed and AEE expectations were that construction was imminent, but this was postponed because of the 1967 War.[7] After Egypt's catastrophic defeat in 1967, government funding was frozen and AEE projects were considered on a theoretical basis alone.

Although the 1967 War led to a drying-up of funds for all nuclear projects, including power plants, a revival of interest in nuclear power was evident after 1970. In that year a new survey carried out jointly by the AEE and the Ministry of Electricity concluded that Egypt would face an electric power shortage of 7,500 MW even after all the country's hydro-electric potential had been exhausted. El Guibaily, who was associated with this new survey, said the deficit could be met by constructing nuclear power plants. He was vague about the number of nuclear plants that could be constructed, but he did point out that new economies of scale in nuclear technology made nuclear power stations competitive with thermal ones.

El Guibaily's conclusions were presented to the fourth United Nations International Conference on the Peaceful Uses of Atomic Energy, held in Geneva in May 1971.[8] His opinions were corroborated by an IAEA-sponsored market survey for nuclear power in Egypt.[9] This survey estimated that Egypt would require an additional 6,000 MW of installed electrical capacity between 1980 and 1990, a gap that nuclear power could help to fill. The 1971 Geneva Conference also provided a forum for discussing other peaceful uses of nuclear technology. El Guibaily's presentation discusses, for instance, the use of nuclear power for desalination. The desalination project, similar to the proposal made by Hedayat's DCA, was taken up and discussed by another member of the AEE, Dr H.Y. Fouad.[10] His conclusion was that nuclear-powered desalination plants would prove too costly to build.

El Guibaily's other major contribution to the 1971 Conference was the proposal for using nuclear explosives to carry out excavations in remote parts of the country.[11] He said such explosives could be used to blast a canal for connecting Lake Nasser on the Nile with the New Valley in the south-western desert, for a canal linking the Mediterranean to a natural depression in the Western Desert, called Qattara, and finally for stimulating the production of oil and gas wells. These ideas of using nuclear explosives for engineering never went beyond the discussion stage, but using nuclear explosives in the Qattara project remained an attractive idea for years to come. In 1978 a West German feasibility survey dismissed the prospect of using nuclear explosives because they were too unreliable.

The Qattara project has an ancient pedigree stretching back to 1916, when studies were first carried out for filling the depression with sea water over a long period of time and using the difference in elevation between the coast and the depression to generate electric power.[12]

Studies now in hand favour using conventional explosives to blast either tunnels or an open canal between the Mediterranean and Qattara.

THE SEARCH FOR FOREIGN COLLABORATION

From 1955 onwards, when Moscow emerged as Egypt's principal arms supplier, Nasser pinned his hopes on the Soviet Union as the best foreign source for advanced nuclear technology. Students were sent for training to Soviet training centres from 1957, but the Soviet Union also played a major role in setting up the nuclear research centre at Inchas, which included building a small experimental reactor. The advent of a state-sponsored scholarship scheme later enabled students to pursue their postgraduate studies in many other foreign nuclear institutes, including Harwell in England, Saclay in France, Barc in India, and at Argonne and other centres in the United States. Contacts with West German and American companies were important in the period between 1964 and 1967, when Egypt first showed interest in acquiring a nuclear power reactor.

Concern over what the Israelis were doing at Dimona led Nasser to approach the Chinese after 1967 for their help in acquiring sensitive nuclear know-how that would give Egypt a nuclear military option. After the failure of the Peking talks, the Egyptians turned to India. Bilateral nuclear co-operation agreements between Cairo and Delhi go back to 1957. They were mostly concerned with the 'exchange' of scientists, although in practice this was a one-way ticket since most of the traffic was from Egypt to India. An agreement signed between Egypt and India in 1970 was more substantial because it also anticipated joint research in the production of heavy water, nuclear fuels and raw-materials prospecting. In 1973 Sadat asked for Indian assistance in building a 50 MW nuclear desalination plant. Discussions had barely started when President Nixon offered nuclear power reactors to both Egypt and India. The Egyptians then turned cool towards the idea of working with the Indians because they thought the United States would disapprove and its offer of the nuclear power reactors would be withdrawn.

THE 1974 NUCLEAR PROTOCOL WITH THE UNITED STATES

Nixon's state visit to Egypt in 1974 was the start of a new relationship between Cairo and Washington. Nixon had offered two nuclear power plants to Egypt and in 1975 a nuclear agreement was initialled.

In 1976 a letter of intent was issued to Westinghouse to build the first 600 MW PWR on the Alexandrian coast. In 1978 a delegation of American energy experts visited Egypt to make a first-hand assessment of the country's energy needs. The delegation noted that projections for nuclear generating capacity by the year 2000 varied from 6,000 MW to 12,000 MW. 'Beyond 2000 a rapid expansion in the use of nuclear or advanced energy systems will be needed unless gas and oil can be significantly increased above current production targets.'[13] However, the delegation's visit did not stimulate the expected new era of nuclear co-operation between Washington and Cairo.

The bilateral agreement initialled in 1975 was first abandoned, then renegotiated and finally initialled again, and signed only in 1981. There were three reasons for the delay. The Indian nuclear test of 1974 led to a revision of US nuclear legislation, which in turn meant the renegotiation of all existing bilateral nuclear co-operation agreements. The change of Administrations from Nixon to Ford and then to Carter also contributed to the delay. A third reason was that until 1980 the Egyptians were unable to raise the money to pay for the first nuclear power station, estimated to cost between US$600 million and $800 million.

There was still another reason for the delay. In 1979, when the nuclear co-operation agreement was being renegotiated with Washington, the Egyptians startled the Americans by proposing that any safeguards included in the new agreement should be considered suspended in the event of a new war breaking out in the Middle East. Since this proposal ran counter to the spirit of US nuclear legislation — as well as to the NPT — the talks were abruptly suspended. The Americans did not know that in the same period, 1974 to 1979, Egypt had been holding secret talks with French companies to improve the country's nuclear research centre. These discussions, revealed for the first time in this book, were with the state-backed Technicatome company to upgrade the Inchas reactor from 2 MW to 10 MW.

In 1976 Technicatome was asked once again if it would upgrade the reactor and also build a prototype fuel-fabrication plant at Inchas. Technicatome came up with a Fr50 million proposal to do both jobs, but backed away at the last moment under pressure from Paris. This was the period when Paris was conducting an aggressive nuclear exports drive, which included the sale of reactors to Iraq and a reprocessing plant to Pakistan. In 1977 discussion began with a private French engineering company, Robatel, to build two radio-active 'hot cells' at Inchas. The hot cells were duly installed in 1982 to give Egyptian scientists experience of nuclear waste management.

RATIFYING THE NPT

The failure to reach an agreement with Technicatome, as well as with the United States in 1979, led to a rethinking of strategy. In 1980 the Ministries of Electricity and Oil Production argued in a joint memorandum that the country's energy options were so limited that nuclear energy was a must, and ratifying the NPT was the only way of getting the relevant technology. The Ministry of Foreign Affairs, which held out against ratifying the NPT until Israel did so, was finally brought around to see that economic necessity had to prevail.

THE AFTERMATH OF RATIFICATION

In late December 1980 Sadat announced the imminent ratification of the NPT. The instruments of ratification were signed the following February in London.[14] Earlier that month, following a private visit to Paris by Sadat, the French and Egyptians signed an agreement on nuclear co-operation that provided for two French PWR plants to be built at Al Daaba, 160 miles west of Alexandria.[15] The previous Burg El Arab/Sidi Kreir site was all but abandoned because of environmentalist objections. Before signing the agreement with France, Sadat said he was setting aside a portion of the government's oil revenues to pay for the eight nuclear plants planned for by the end of the century. This was in keeping with the Ministry of Electricity's new strategy of installing 8,000 MW of nuclear generating power, 35 per cent of the country's electricity consumption, by the end of the century.[16]

Ratifying the NPT also cleared the way in March 1981 for the successful conclusion of a bilateral nuclear agreement with the United States. The Egyptians hoped that American companies would build two or more nuclear power stations — with a combined output of 2000 MW — either along the Mediterranean coast or along the Red Sea. Tenders for the remaining four plants were thrown open to interested bidders, with applications invited from West German and British companies.

In the event, these hopes of a new nuclear age dawning in Egypt proved to be premature. Falling oil prices and higher nuclear costs affected Egypt's energy policy after 1983. French companies submitting tenders for the Al Daaba reactors were asked to delay their applications for financial reasons.[17] In 1984 Electricity Minister Maher Abaza announced that plans to build eight nuclear power stations by the end of the century would be delayed by at least five years because of problems in finding financial backing.[18] Egypt's hopes of becoming the leading civil nuclear power in the Middle East were indefinitely postponed.

NOTES

1. Robert Stephens, *Nasser, a political biography* (Allen Lane, London, 1971), pp. 316–17.

2. Shai Feldman, *Israeli nuclear deterrence* (Columbia University Press, New York, 1982), p. 12.

3. The *Guardian*, 4 May 1964.

4. A.B. Zahlan, *Science and science policy in the Arab world* (Croom Helm, London, 1979), pp. 35–6.

5. Professor Mohammed El Naadi, interview with the author, 1981.

6. The *Christian Science Monitor*, 30 June 1967.

7. See, for example, M.E. El Fouly and J.K. Snape, *Organisation for a nuclear power project* (UAE AEE Report no. 41, 1967).

8. M.A. El Koshairy, El Guibaily *et al. Possibilities of introducing and integrating nuclear power in the Egyptian power system*, A/Conf., 49/P/137, Geneva, 1971.

9. Egypt, *Marketing survey for nuclear power in developing countries* (IAEA, Vienna, September 1973).

10. H.Y. Fouad, *Optimisation of natural uranium heavy moderated reactors for desalination* (Atomkernenergie (ATKE), Bd. 23, 1974).

11. El Guibaily *et al.*, 'Prospects of peaceful applications of nuclear explosions in the United Arab Republic', A/Conf., 49/P/144, Geneva, 1971.

12. *Qattara Depression*, introduced by Almed Sultan Ismail, Cairo (Egyptian Ministry of Electricity and Energy, 1978).

13. United States Department of Energy, *Joint Egypt-US Report, in Egypt/US Co-operative Energy Assessment* (Washington, April 1979).

14. 26 February 1981. A statement released by the Egyptian Foreign Ministry said Egypt's ratification of the NPT stemmed from its belief in the necessity of limiting the spread of nuclear weapons. Egypt, the statement went on to say, expected wholehearted support and assistance for its nuclear programme from industrialised countries with developed nuclear industries.

15. Joint Franco-Egyptian statement on nuclear co-operation, Paris, 12 February 1981.

16. *Strategy of Ministry of Electricity and Energy for the period 1980-2000* Cairo, December 1980).

17. *Financial Times*, 5 April 1983.

18. *Financial Times*, 4 September 1984.

5

Libya

Colonel Muammar Qadhafi of Libya, described by the late President
Sadat as a 'madman barking in his tent', is the number one bogeyman
of the Middle East. His support for numerous terrorist organisations,
ranging from the Japanese Red Army to Baader Meinhof and various
Palestinian groups, and his attempts to destabilise the regimes of
neighbouring countries like Chad, seemingly confirm the image he
has created for himself.

Almost from the day the Libyan monarchy was toppled, Qadhafi
has also sought to purchase or manufacture a nuclear bomb that would
add to the prestige of his Green Revolution and enhance his personal
status. Frustrated so far in his bid to make Libya a nuclear power,
he has unsuccessfully tried to attack the nuclear research centre at
Dimona, Israel, which stands as a permanent reminder of his own
nuclear inadequacy. In 1981 Libya's ambassador in Jordan, Mr Aziz
Shenib, was personally instructed by Qadhafi to obtain a Syrian rocket,
transfer it secretly to the mountains of eastern Jordan, and fire it at
Dimona.[1] Shenib, who has since defected, said Qadhafi's aim was
not just to hit the reactor, but to knock out the whole area.

Qadhafi's obsession with nuclear weaponry is the theme of this
chapter, which examines the evolution of the Libyan leader's nuclear
aims. One special point of interest, discussed here for the first time,
is Libya's continuing links with Egyptian scientists of high calibre,
despite the poor relations between Tripoli and Cairo. These links were
forged in the early 1970s when Egypt had all but given up hope of
matching the Israeli nuclear effort. This resulted in a transfer of ideas
and manpower to Libya and in retrospect represents the first pan-Arab
bid to mount a challenge to Israel's nuclear dominance. The Egyptian nuclear scientists who went to Libya in the early days of the
Qadhafi-led *coup d'état* believed that there was a real chance of Libya

financing a dual-purpose nuclear power plant. Others were recruited later to plug the gap created by Libya's still-inadequate manpower. If relations between Cairo and Tripoli should improve in the future, these scientists could provide the basis as well of a revival in nuclear co-operation.

The Libyan government claims it is not interested in nuclear weapons and points to its signature on the Nuclear Non-Proliferation Treaty as evidence of good faith. Signature of the NPT, however, is a cover behind which Qadhafi hides his desperate nuclear ambitions. A truer picture of Libya's nuclear aims has emerged from the trial of former CIA agent Edwin Wilson, who pretended to have access to nuclear weapons on the black market and offered to sell them to the Libyans.[2] One of Wilson's associates, a Belgian arms dealer called Armand Donnay, claimed to have access to fissionable material that could be used for making a nuclear bomb. Donnay's offer was discussed with Libyan officials, who asked him what was the 'purity' of his nuclear material. When Donnay told them it was 20 per cent (unsuitable for weapons), a senior Libyan official told him, 'That's no good for us. We need 80 per cent. If you can't do any better than this, then we have no business.'[3]

As a recent analysis by the Carnegie Endowment for International Peace points out, the Wilson episode provides strong evidence 'that the Libyans were seriously interested in buying nuclear arms by clandestine means'.[4]

THE EGYPTIAN LINK

Nuclear co-operation between Libya and Egypt, although now suspended, casts a fascinating perspective on the history of the nuclear arms race in the Middle East. The links with Cairo stem from Egypt's failure to create its own satisfactory nuclear infrastructure. This led in turn to efforts by Salah Hedayat, then Nasser's scientific adviser, to explore the possibility of using Libyan money to keep up the momentum of research and development at Inchas and elsewhere in the country. For this he had the personal backing of both Qadhafi and Nasser.

Hedayat chose to promote such co-operation through a private company, Design Consultants Association (DCA), which he founded in 1965 after resigning from both the Cabinet and the Atomic Energy Establishment. The advantage of using a company like DCA was that it would attract less attention from outside the two countries and, if properly funded, would function as an autonomous body — a kind of Arab nuclear group — that would not be adversely affected by political changes. These hopes were short-lived, however: in 1974, when relations between Libya and Egypt plummetted to an all-time low, following the discovery of a Libyan-backed plot against Sadat, the DCA and its projects were among the early casualties.

The end of formal nuclear co-operation between Libya and Egypt was a bitter personal blow to Hedayat, who had earlier left the Egyptian AEE in 1965 to pursue his nuclear dreams more effectively from outside government. For four years he concentrated his efforts on building up the DCA. In 1970, when a bemused Nasser agreed to form a federation government with Libya, Hedayat was appointed Federation Minister of Scientific Co-operation. The Federation job could have been just a sinecure, but Hedayat saw it as an opportunity to bring his DCA projects to life. Qadhafi, however, was in a hurry. He agreed that Hedayat had a solid plan for building a nuclear infra-structure, from which both Egypt and Libya could benefit, but he also wanted quick results.

In 1970 the Libyan Prime Minister, Major Abdul Salam Jalloud, was dispatched via Cairo to Peking to purchase nuclear weapons. According to Nasser's confidant, journalist Hassanein Heykal, the Egyptian leader warned Jalloud that buying a bomb was not that easy. Jalloud is supposed to have replied, 'Oh, we don't want a big atomic bomb, just a tactical one.' The Chinese predictably refused to sell the Libyans even a 'small' bomb, although they promised to help with nuclear training.[5] As personal relations between the two men soured, so also did the hopes of nuclear collaboration between the two countries. Funds never did materialise for the 40 MW dual-purpose nuclear reactor, although discussions about it continued right up until the end of 1973.

A Libyan-backed plot to kill Sadat was the final nail in the coffin of the short-lived Federation Government. Hedayat resigned soon afterwards and went off to live in semi-retirement at his home in the Heliopolis suburb of Cairo; but he kept up his personal contacts with the Libyans and helped many Egyptian scientists to find work in Tripoli. Some found work in the science departments of Al Fatah University in Tripoli. They included the plasma scientist Dr Eizzat Abdel Aziz, who left Tripoli at the end of 1980 to take up a new appointment as head of Inchas. During his six years in Libya he was Qadhafi's chief nuclear adviser and helped to negotiate agreements with the French and Soviet governnments. He also started up the Plasma Physics Department at Al Fatah University. Other Egyptian scientists who took up jobs in Libya included Dr Galal Zaki, a reactor engineer from Inchas, Dr Ibrahim Dakhli, former head of the metallurgy department at Inchas, Dr Abdel Gawad, a Soviet-trained nuclear chemist, and two plasma physicists, Dr Ahmed Youssef and Dr Mohammed Masood.

EXAMINING THE OPTIONS: NUCLEAR BOMBS OR NUCLEAR TECHNOLOGY

Qadhafi's nuclear strategy had been a two-pronged effort to buy a nuclear bomb 'off the shelf', while simultaneously building a nuclear fuel cycle that would yield the nuclear materials for a bomb. Approaches were made to the Chinese in 1970, as we have seen, and later also to the French, to purchase nuclear weapons. Inevitably, Qadhafi laid himself open to foreign adventurers like Wilson, who tried to bluff him into buying their non-existent weapons. The other half of the strategy was implicit in what Egypt's Hedayat had suggested, which was to build up the country's own scientific infrastructure. This was the building-block mentality that suffered a setback when the Federation Government with Egypt collapsed at the end of 1974.

It was in this period that Qadhafi found another foreign collaborator, Pakistan, which was reeling from the impact of the Indian nuclear test of May 1974. Contact between Qadhafi and Pakistan's Bhutto, discussed in Chapter 8, resulted in a Libyan offer to subsidise the Pakistani nuclear programme. The amount of Libyan money that actually went into Pakistan remains a closely guarded secret, although one conservative estimate is US$100 million. In return, the Libyans wanted access to Pakistan's nuclear programme, with particular emphasis on plutonium-reprocessing and uranium enrichment. The agreement with Pakistan seems to have lapsed after Bhutto's execution, although there have periodically been attempts to revive it.[6] According to Egyptian nuclear scientists who have worked in Libya, there was a steady increase in the number of Pakistani nuclear scientists visiting Libya from 1975 onwards.

The two-pronged Libyan strategy continued to operate even after a nuclear agreement was successfully concluded with Pakistan. In the spring of 1976 the international scientific community was awash with rumours that Qadhafi had placed US$1 million in gold in a Swiss bank account. This was the fee that would be paid to anyone who could give Qadhafi his precious nuclear bomb.

AGREEMENTS WITH OTHER COUNTRIES

In 1974 an agreement was signed with Argentina to promote the peaceful uses of nuclear energy.[7] According to this agreement Argentina was to help Libya with the front end of the fuel cycle, which involved the prospecting for uranium and its processing. Later, under pressure from the United States, Argentina slowed down the implementation of the agreement.

The Libyans also left their nuclear calling cards with France, with whom an agreement was signed in 1976. The French were unwilling to part with a nuclear bomb, but there was interest in selling Qadhafi a reactor. French Prime Minister Jacques Chirac, who also negotiated the Osiris agreement with Iraq, visited Libya in March 1976, when he proposed the sale of a research reactor.[8] He also discussed the possibility of selling Libya a 600 MW nuclear power reactor, but both projects were later shelved.

The most promising offer of assistance was from the Soviet Union. Soviet Prime Minister Alexei Kosygin visited Tripoli in 1975, which led to an agreement for building a nuclear research centre at Tajora, near Tripoli, and the construction of a small 10 MW research reactor.[9] In return, the Soviet Union insisted that Libya ratify the NPT. Negotiations have recently been revived over the additional building of two nuclear power reactors.

In 1978 the Libyans turned to India to see what nuclear assistance they could obtain from Delhi. Major Jalloud, who visited Delhi in 1978, promised to sell Libyan oil to the Indians on concessionary terms in return for help in building a complete nuclear fuel cycle. The Indians were taken aback. According to eye-witness accounts, Jalloud made his proposition directly to Prime Minister Desai. Desai explained that building a nuclear fuel cycle was a complex operation, and moreover, that India, which had its own requirements to consider, was not in the market for selling major items of nuclear technology. Jalloud reached inside the breast pocket of his jacket, pulled out a cheque book and asked Desai to name his price. When the Indian leader still proved unwilling, Jalloud told him that he knew of other countries that would respond more positively.[10]

A memorandum of understanding was signed with Jalloud before he left, but the Indians tried to keep it as vague as possible. A group of Indian scientists visited Libya in 1979 and they reported that Libya had to do much more to improve the quality of its scientific manpower. In the words of one member of the delegation, Libya's nuclear experts consisted of 'one mathematician, one zoologist and one failed botanist'. The Indians' reluctance to give Qadhafi what he wanted had its repercussions, however. Jalloud never fulfilled his part of the agreement to sell India two million tons of oil at favourable rates.

In the 1980s Libya tried unsuccessfully to revive its nuclear agreement with Argentina,[11] and contacts were also established with Brazil. In 1985 attempts were made to purchase nuclear services from Belgium, but Brussels cancelled a US$1,000 million nuclear trade pact under pressure from Washington.[12]

THE PROBLEM OF MANPOWER

Although some progress has been made in training scientists, Libya still suffers from a shortage of skilled scientific manpower. The Libyans cannot compare themselves with Pakistan, for example, where one centre alone, the enrichment plant at Kahuta, employs 3,000 scientists and technicians.

The Libyan Atomic Energy Commission continues to depend on Libyan and other foreign experts, who it is able to attract with high salaries. Foreign scientists have helped to run the Department of Nuclear and Electronic Engineering at Al Fatah University. The Department only issued its first undergraduate degrees in 1982. Efforts to train Libyan students abroad have been only partially successful. Some students were sent to the Soviet Union in 1977 for training in metallurgy and nuclear engineering, but the United States was the preferred destination. In 1978 there were more than 100 Libyans studying nuclear engineering at American universities, but by 1981 this number had been halved. As relations with Washington deteriorated, the United States grew reluctant to accept Libyan students for training in the nuclear sciences. An informal ban has been operating ever since then.

Qadhafi has only himself to blame for this situation. His well-known interest in nuclear weapons has denied students access to 'dangerous' learning. There was considerable alarm in 1978 when Mr Ahmed El Shahati, head of the Libyan Foreign Liaison Office, told Dr Jeremy Stone, Director of the Federation of American Scientists, that his government was interested in nuclear weapons.[13] Whether Shahati was being unduly naïve by trying to score a propaganda point, or whether he made his comments in an unguarded moment, his views triggered off alarms within the American scientific community. After returning home to the United States, Stone wrote to Soviet ambassador Anatoly Dobrynin and suggested that his government reconsider its nuclear agreements with Tripoli. Ever since then the Soviet Union has been slow in implementing its nuclear agreements with Libya; and since 1978 Qadhafi's officials have been less prepared to boast of their interest in nuclear weaponry.

In October 1981 the Libyan-funded Arab Development Institute of Beirut hosted a conference on nuclear technology in developing countries. In his keynote address at the start of the conference, which was held in northern Italy, the Institute's Director, Dr Ali Ben El Ashar, declared:[14]

> Contrary to the distorted image given by some news media, we do not manufacture weaponry of death and destruction . . . We are just a small country trying to make the best of its resources for its own future and the Arab nations' future.

ORGANISATION AND RESEARCH

Libya's Atomic Energy Commission, founded in 1973, is a grand-sounding body that in reality consists of only a dozen of the country's leading scientists. They include the Director-General, Dr Abdel Fateh Eskangi, a Yugoslav-trained nuclear chemist, Dr Fateh Nouh, an American-trained nuclear engineer, and Dr Ibrahim Hussairi, an American-trained nuclear physicist in charge of Tajora.

The AEC's main task is to run the US$400 million nuclear research centre at Tajora, east of Tripoli, constructed entirely with Soviet help. In Tajora Soviet experts have built laboratories for nuclear metallurgy, nuclear chemistry, nuclear physics and plasma physics. A 10 MW research reactor due to be commissioned in 1981 is believed to be functioning. Other responsibilities of the AEC include uranium prospecting and planning for nuclear power plants. Tentative agreement was reached with the Soviet Union for two 440 MW reactors at Sirte, but this project, despite the revival of the nuclear agreement with the Soviet Union, has not advanced beyond the planning stage.

THE FUTURE

Qadhafi's nuclear ambitions have resulted in the most expensive nuclear research centre in the Arab world. The US$400 million Tajora site, with its research reactor and laboratories of plasma physics, nuclear physics, chemistry and metallurgy, easily compares with Inchas in Egypt or Towaitha in Iraq; but the Libyans are still light years away from making their own nuclear bomb. They still lack an integrated nuclear fuel cycle that would yield nuclear material for bombs, and the number of trained nuclear scientists is still low. The Soviet Union has been Libya's principal source of nuclear technology, but Moscow exercises strict control of nuclear sales and would not be a party to weapons-building efforts.

Qadhafi has tried to use the country's oil money to buy nuclear technology, but this has not been as successful as he would have liked. His best hope now lies in persuading Pakistan to part with its nuclear secrets in return for the money that Qadhafi gave Bhutto more than a decade ago. Pakistan, as Chapter 8 will indicate, has mastered uranium-enrichment technology and has been testing the components of a nuclear bomb. What blandishments can Qadhafi or any other Arab leader now offer to Islamabad in return for sharing in Pakistan's nuclear achievement?

NOTES

1. David Blundy and Andrew Lycett, *Qaddafi and the Libyan revolution* (Weidenfeld and Nicolson, London, 1987).

2. Joseph C. Goulden, *The death merchant* (Sidgwick and Jackson, London, 1985), pp. 310–13.

3. Ibid.

4. Leonard S. Spector, *Going nuclear* (Carnegie Endowment, Cambridge, MA, 1987), p. 151.

5. Mohammed Heikal, *The road to Ramadan* (Collins, London, 1975), p. 76.

6. For example, see *The Economist* Foreign Report, *Libya's nuclear dreams*, 9 July 1981.

7. The *Sunday Times*, 11 May 1975.

8. The *Guardian*, 23 March 1971.

9. BBC Summary of World Broadcasts, Soviet Union, 18 February 1976.

10. Interviews with the author, Atomic Energy Commission, Bombay, September 1978.

11. Spector, *Going nuclear*, p. 149.

12. Ibid.

13. The *Daily Telegraph*, 7 December 1978.

14. Grado Nuclear Technology Conference, Italy, October 1981.

6

Iraq

Iraq's nuclear programme is at a standstill. French promises to repair the Osiraq reactor, bombed by Israeli war planes in June 1981, have not been fulfilled. Similarly, a Soviet proposal to build Iraq's first nuclear power plant[1] has been agreed but not implemented. The country's nuclear research centre at Towaitha, 17 miles south of Baghdad, lies in ruins, a bitter memorial to the Arab world's best hope of acquiring weapons-grade nuclear material.

According to American sources, Iraq remains interested in nuclear arms, and recently, following the example of Libya, tried to purchase nuclear material (plutonium) on the black market.[2] Baghdad also retains control over a small amount of highly enriched uranium, which was purchased as fuel for Osiraq, but Iraq's long-term strength lies in her body of trained scientists and her oil purchasing power which, when the Gulf War ends, will revive her bargaining power with international nuclear suppliers. The Iraqis maintain to this day that they had no intention of making nuclear weapons and point to membership of the NPT as proof of their sincerity. Yet as the distinguished American analyst Leonard Spector has pointed out, Iraq has also ratified the 1925 Geneva Protocol against chemical weapons. Iraq's continued violations of the Protocol 'raise fundamental questions as to the strength of its other arms control commitments'.[3]

This chapter examines Iraq's strategy for buying the vital components of a nuclear fuel cycle that would have given Baghdad access to plutonium. It also considers Israeli fears that Iraq was hell-bent on producing nuclear weapons.

OSIRIS, OSIRAQ OR TAMUZ

When Israeli war planes bombed Iraq's research centre at Towaitha, they destroyed both the powerful French-built Osiraq reactor and President Sadam Hussein's ambitions for turning his country into the Arab world's leading nuclear power. Egypt's faltering efforts to acquire nuclear technology inspired the oil-rich Iraqis and the Libyans to mount their own national nuclear programmes that would win them regional prestige and challenge Israeli supremacy.

But for the Israelis, Iraq today would be the proud owner of the most powerful research reactor in the Arab world. The 70 MW reactor, designed and built by the French state-owned company Technicatome, was named by the company after the Egyptian god, Osiris. Later, taking Iraqi sentiments into account, Technicatome changed the name of the Baghdad-bound reactor to Osiraq. The proud Iraqis changed its name to Tamuz, or July, the month in which an army *coup d'état* overthrew the monarchy of King Feisal.

The Technicatome sales catalogue conveys an artist's impression of a completed Osiris reactor that looks like a domed fuel tank with a solitary chimney-stack projecting upwards from one side. It is a conventional picture of a nuclear reactor. In the foreground is a long, two-storeyed building containing offices and research laboratories.[4] The reactor is described as the latest 'experimental reactor constructed at the Saclay site by the CEA [French Atomic Energy Commission]. Its main purpose is the irradiation under high thermal and fast neutron flux of structural materials intended for electronuclear power stations.' The uranium fuel for running the reactor was enriched to 93 per cent, a high enough grade for weapons. During their negotiations with Iraq, the French agreed to supply in advance some 72 kilograms of this highly enriched uranium, sufficient for more than one nuclear bomb.

Critics of the Franco-Iraqi nuclear co-operation agreement of 1975 concentrated their fire on the composition of the Osiraq fuel elements and the dangers they represented for nuclear proliferation. The Israelis, who were among the first to voice their concern, promptly dubbed the reactor 'O Chirac', a sarcastic tribute to the then French Prime Minister Jacques Chirac, who had carried out the negotiations with the Iraqis. It was Chirac who travelled to Baghdad in 1974 to sign up Fr15 billion of industrial orders, including the nuclear plant. By 1976, with the reactor deal agreed, the French were well-placed to compete for lucrative Iraqi orders. France was also importing nearly 20 per cent of its oil from Iraq at below market prices.

Pressure increased on Paris to amend the original agreement with

Baghdad as the delivery date for Osiris, May 1979, drew nearer. Concern was expressed by Washington, which held the patent for the main French LWR (the Framatome PWR). The United States was also the main source of enriched uranium for France's domestic nuclear power programme. In response to American pressure, the French tried to work out a compromise for the supply of Osiris fuel. The compromise proposed was to change the type of fuel so that it was enriched to only 20 per cent, a level not suitable for weapons. The Iraqis refused, but they did agree that the fuel should be supplied in smaller quantities of 15 kilograms each, instead of one single shipment of 72 kilograms. Baghdad also agreed to allow French scientists to stay on for longer at Towaitha after the reactor was installed.

The type of reactor fuel was only part of the strategic dimension of Osiris, however. 'Blankets' of natural uranium placed around the reactor core would have been a source of plutonium. 'The Osiris reactor is particularly well suited to such a task', according to Israel's Shai Feldman.[5] For this possible route the Iraqis would also have needed sufficient quantities of uranium ore, a fuel-fabrication plant and reprocessing facilities. As we shall see later in the chapter, the Iraqi Atomic Energy Commission was well briefed on these additional requirements.

THE ATOMIC ENERGY COMMISSION

The AEC, established in 1956[6] under the direction of a respected physicist, Dr Mohammed Kital, had the modest objectives of using the atom to serve medicine, agriculture and industry. A nuclear institute was opened shortly afterwards in Baghdad, with specialist sections in nuclear physics, chemistry, radioactive chemistry, biology and agriculture. The institute was later moved to a new site, Towaitha, on the banks of the Tigris.

In 1959, a year after the pro-Western monarchy had been toppled in Baghdad, the first batch of Towaitha students was sent to the Soviet Union for further training. Moscow accepted 375 students. In 1961 an agreement was signed to build a 2 MW experimental reactor, identical to the one that was also given to Egypt, at Towaitha. The reactor was commissioned in 1965. For the next ten years the AEC concentrated on improving the quality of scientific manpower within the country. Science departments at Iraqi universities were strengthened and students were encouraged to go abroad for further training.

A geological survey established in 1966 used Soviet help to survey radioactive mineral deposits along the borders with Syria, Iran and Turkey. The Soviets were particularly helpful with training nuclear scientists, but students were also sent to the West and to India, which had a vigorous programme of nuclear research. The Indian nuclear physicist Dr Raja Ramanna, who remembers training Iraqi students at the Bhabha Atomic Research Centre (BARC) near Bombay, described them as very hard-working and totally committed to their research. He said that they were far more impressive than any other Arab students he had ever met.[7]

Two Iraqi scientists who benefited from their government's generous overseas scholarship schemes were a physicist and a chemist. Dr Hussain Al Shahristani, a nuclear chemist, was trained at the Universities of London and Toronto. Dr Jaafar Dhia Jaafar, a nuclear physicist, trained at Imperial College, London. Shahristani, who became director of radiochemistry research at Towaitha in 1970 and later scientific adviser to the President, was arrested in 1979 after taking part in anti-government demonstrations organised by Islamic fundamentalist groups. According to Amnesty International, he was subsequently seen in the Al Rashid military hospital in Baghdad, where he was taken after being tortured.[8] Jaafar, appointed head of nuclear physics at Towaitha, was taken into custody after he wrote to President Hussein, asking why Shahristani had been arrested.

Sharistani and Jaafar are both members of the majority Shia sect that is opposed to the Baath government in Baghdad. After they were arrested, an Israeli nuclear expert familiar with their work said Israel was fortunate that Iraq's two best nuclear scientists had been arrested.

PLANS FOR EXPANSION AFTER 1975

The agreement for Osiraq and its controversial fuel rightly attracted the most attention abroad, but it distracted attention from Iraq's equally controversial bid to create a plutonium cycle by purchasing uranium ore, fuel-fabrication and reprocessing facilities. There were negotiations with the Italians to buy another reactor still, a 40 MW heavy-water type, that fitted in beautifully with a plutonium strategy. For a country like Iraq, with no nuclear power strategy, the decision to harness an entire nuclear fuel cycle was staggering. It could not be justified on economic grounds, as Iraq's oil reserves are second only to Saudi Arabia's. Inevitably, the suspicion was that Baghdad was trying to create nuclear military options as quickly as possible.

The plutonium strategy was based on close co-operation with

Italy which, although it lacked the aggressive export instincts of France, had the technology that Iraq wanted. Contacts with the Italians were established in 1975, when Iraq hosted a conference on the peaceful uses of atomic energy for scientific and economic development. In 1979 a high-powered delegation from Rome, headed by the Chairman of the Italian Atomic Energy Commission (CNEN), Professor Enzio Clemental, visited Baghdad. This visit facilitated contacts between the Iraqi AEC and a private Italian company, Snia Techint, which specialised in nuclear technology.

Snia agreed to sell Iraq equipment for a radiochemistry laboratory, which could be used for small-scale reprocessing, a fuel-fabrication plant and two other laboratories for studying heat phenomena and medical isotopes.[9] The Italians also agreed to train 100 Iraqi technicians. In 1981, before Towaitha was attacked by Israel, the Iraqis were negotiating with another Italian company, Ansaldo, for a 40 MW experimental reactor that had been developed only as a prototype.[10] Cirene was a heavy-water experimental reactor that used natural uranium for fuel. It would have been ideal for producing plutonium, but negotiations were suspended after the Osiris bombing.

RAW MATERIALS

The fuel for an adapted form of Osiris, or for Cirene — if agreement had been reached — was natural uranium. Earlier geological surveys carried out with Soviet, French and Indian assistance had determined that Iraq's own uranium reserves were modest and of low-grade quality. Thus, in 1979, agreements for purchasing uranium were signed with Portugal and Brazil.[11] Both countries were importers of Iraqi oil. The more significant agreement was with Brazil, which was a comprehensive nuclear agreement covering the exchange of scientists between the two countries and the export of Brazilian uranium to Iraq.

SAFEGUARDS

International concern about Iraq's nuclear investment was fended off by Baghdad's referring to its treaty obligations under the NPT and IAEA safeguards that would prevent the misuse of imported technology. As we have seen earlier in the chapter, Iraq's abuse of the 1925 Geneva Protocol on chemical weapons raises doubts about

Baghdad's commitment to other treaties such as the NPT.

The issue of IAEA safeguards, as set out in the NPT, was another matter. In 1980, one year before the Osiris raid, the IAEA spent US$25 million annually on safeguards. In 1980 the Agency's 150 inspectors looked at 500 facilities in 50 countries. Film and video cameras were installed and a total of six million pictures taken. Three million seals were fixed to make sure there was no diversion of nuclear material when the inspectors were not looking.

Yet despite these impressive statistics, the adequacy of safeguards has been questioned more than once. Mr Enrico Jacchia, a former head of European nuclear safeguards, warned: 'it is unreasonable . . . and dangerous to let people believe that nuclear safeguards have become adequate instruments to prevent the proliferation of nuclear weapons. The ways to cheat the international safeguards are as numerous as the ways of the Lord.'[12] Within the Agency itself there were long debates about how effective the safeguards for Osiris could be. The head of the IAEA's nuclear inspectorate claimed that his inspectors would swiftly detect any diversion of Osiris fuel or any attempt to make plutonium by placing natural uranium blankets around the core, but at least one group of inspectors believed the opposite.[13]

Even if the system of safeguards were perfect, there was little the Agency could do once diversion or misuse of materials was detected. One of the shortcomings of the NPT is that it still provides for no agreed system of sanctions once a government violates the Treaty. If a serious diversion were discovered, for example, the Agency board would pass on its findings to the UN Security Council and at that point consider its job finished. Senior Agency aides described their job as similar to a fire alarm: 'We are the alarm that shouts fire. After that it's up to them [the Security Council] to decide what thickness of hose is required, how much water is needed.'[14]

SABOTAGE

Doubts about Iraq's nuclear motives led to a series of incidents of sabotage and murder aimed at slowing down the country's nuclear programme. On 6 April 1979 saboteurs entered a warehouse in the Mediterranean port of Seyne-sur-Mer, near Toulon, and blew up the reactor cores of Osiris that were awaiting shipment to Baghdad. The precision with which the saboteurs carried out their work suggested that it was an 'inside' job. Although a self-proclaimed French ecological group claimed responsibility,[15] no French environmentalist had ever heard of them before. It was more likely to have been carried out by sympathetic elements of French intelligence working with agents of the legendary Israeli secret service, Mossad. Shortly afterwards, an Israeli spokesman told the press in Paris: 'This will delay the Iraqis by a year and a half.'[16]

There was ample evidence that the Israelis were worried. In 1980, when the Osiris reactor cores were being repaired, Israel's Yuval Neeman warned that Baghdad would be capable of producing a nuclear bomb within a year, and General Zipori, the Deputy Defence Minister, said studies were being conducted to see how Iraq could be prevented from becoming a nuclear power.[17] In Britain Winston Churchill MP added his voice to the concern that was being expressed in Israel by criticising the Franco-Iraqi reactor deal. 'France in its lust for oil appears to have thrown away all constraints of morality, good sense or even self-interest', he wrote in *The Times*.[18]

In 1980 the campaign of sabotage which had started with the explosion at Seyne-sur-Mer turned to murder when a nuclear engineer employed by the Iraqi AEC was found bludgeoned to death in his Paris hotel room. There was no evidence to link the Seyne-sur-Mer explosion with the Paris murder of Dr Yahya El Meshad, but at the time both incidents were interpreted as a warning to Iraq not to proceed with its nuclear plans. Dr Meshad, employed by the Iraqi AEC since 1976, was in Paris on official business in June 1980. On the evening before he was due to return home to Baghdad, he was seen dining with friends at a fashionable restaurant. A few hours later he was found murdered in room 1074 of the Meridien Hotel in Paris.

Was Meshad's death a warning?; or was he carrying information that was of value to Iraq's enemies? There was certainly nothing of interest in his academic background that would attract his murderers. He was born in Egypt in 1932, where he trained as an electrical engineer. Later he spent two years in Moscow (1971–2) where he trained as a nuclear engineer. In 1975, before accepting a better-paid teaching job at Baghdad University — to be followed by a contract with the Iraqi AEC — he was head of nuclear engineering at Alexandria University.

Meshad's secrets, whatever they were, died with him, but attacks, sometimes followed by warning letters, continued against French and Italian companies selling nuclear components to Iraq. Responsibility was claimed by a previously unknown Committee to Safeguard the Islamic Revolution.[19] Warning letters from the Committee continued into 1981, sometimes addressed to the families of French scientists working at the Osiris site at Towaitha.

IRAQ RESPONDS TO OSIRIS FEARS

Throughout 1979 the Iraqis refused to respond to mounting international controversy about their nuclear purchases. There was no counter-propaganda campaign, no invitation to foreign journalists to see for themselves what was taking shape at Towaitha, no attempt to enlist the moral support of other Third World countries. In March 1980 the Iraqi Ministry of Foreign Affairs finally issued a terse statement:[20]

> The campaign waged by the USA against the technological co-operation between Iraq and each of France and Italy, showed its continuing hostility to Iraq and the Arab nation . . . A spokesman for the Foreign Ministry told the Iraqi News Agency that the United States aimed from the campaign to gain election support by begging Zionist votes at the expense of the people's freedom and independence.

The Iraqi President addressed himself to the nuclear issue in August 1980, two months after Meshad was murdered in Paris. President Hussein told foreign journalists in Baghdad that his country was not planning to make nuclear weapons. During a two-hour speech, heavily laden with sarcasm, he said:[21]

> These Arabs, the Zionists said, could do nothing but ride camels, cry over the ruins of their houses and sleep in tents. Two years ago the Zionists and their supporters came up with a declaration that Iraq was about to produce the atom bomb. But how could a people who only knew how to ride camels produce an atomic bomb?

Hussein's determination to press ahead with the nuclear programme, despite an international campaign of intimidation, set in motion the Israeli plan to destroy Osiris for good. In July 1980 an Israeli minister said that studies were being conducted to prevent Iraq from becoming a nuclear power, and it is probable that Jerusalem made plans to attack Osiris later the same year.

However, the start of the Gulf War in September 1980, followed by an Iranian air raid against Towaitha, interfered with the planned attack. Israeli Prime Minister Begin, who had an election looming the following year, may also have decided to delay the attack for political reasons until June 1981.

The Israelis still have no hard evidence of an Iraqi nuclear weapons strategy, although a military option would inevitably be created as the country's nuclear infrastructure was built up. Until the Towaitha raid the only published evidence of Iraq's desire for nuclear weapons was contained in an ambiguous interview of Saddam Hussein in a Beirut publication. Hussein reportedly described his country's nuclear programme as the first Arab attempt at nuclear arming.[22] After the Israeli attack an understandably enraged President Hussein called on the Arab world to develop nuclear weapons in order to balance Israel's nuclear capability.

The Israelis were not the only ones to worry about Iraq's nuclear intentions, since Iranian war planes had also bombed Towaitha one year earlier. The two attacks lowered the threshold of nuclear weapons proliferation by identifying civil nuclear projects as strategic targets. International safeguards agreed as part of the NPT are meant to prevent the misuse of civil nuclear technology. Yet the Iranian and Israeli raids implied profound mistrust of such safeguards. Such reasoning, if it is accepted by other countries, has far-reaching implications, because it jeopardises the safety of all nuclear installations, whether civil or military.

After the Towaitha raid no country can assume that an interest in nuclear technology will be accepted at face value as an investment intended purely and simply for generating electric power. The dividing line between the civil and military uses of nuclear technology has become much harder to sustain.

NOTES

1. *International Herald Tribune*, 24 March 1984.
2. Leonard Spector, *Going nuclear* (Carnegie Endowment, Cambridge, MA, 1987), p. 163.
3. Ibid, pp. 160-1.
4. Technicatome, *A complete range of experimental reactors*.
5. Shai Feldman, *Israeli nuclear deterrence* (Columbia University Press, New York, 1982), p. 76.
6. *Al Thawrah* (Baghdad), 10 February 1975.
7. Interview with the author, Bombay, July 1978.
8. Amnesty International, *Case of three Iraqi scientists imprisoned in Baghdad* (MDE, 14/21/80).
9. *International Herald Tribune*, 20 March 1980.
10. *La Repubblica* (Rome), 28 July 1980.
11. *Financial Times*, 9 January 1980 and 28 March 1980.
12. The *Observer*, 16 June 1981.

13. Ibid.
14. Ibid.
15. Steve Weissman and Herbert Krosney, *The Islamic bomb* (Times Books, New York, 1981), p. 230.
16. Ibid, p. 231.
17. The *Daily Telegraph*, 19 July 1980.
18. *The Times*, 11 July 1980.
19. Weissman and Krosney, *The Islamic bomb*, p. 243.
20. *Baghdad Observer*, 21 March 1980.
21. *The Times*, 21 July 1980.
22. Weissman and Krosney, *The Islamic bomb*, p. 89.

7

Iran

Revolutionary Iran lacks the technological ability to make nuclear weapons, but key members of the regime have expressed a definite interest in acquiring them. A former energy adviser to the late Shah of Iran has disclosed in a recent interview[1] that he was ordered to build a nuclear bomb. Mr Fereidun Fesharaki, who has since defected to the West, claims he was told in May 1979 by one of Ayatollah Khomeini's advisers: 'It is your duty to build this bomb. Our civilisation is in danger and we have to do it.' A study by the Carnegie Endowment for International Peace also claims that the Shah initiated a secret nuclear weapons project that was interrupted by the Khomeini revolution.[2] This project existed in parallel with a declared policy of harnessing nuclear power for peaceful purposes to develop alternative sources of energy.

Iran has three possible routes to the bomb. It can try to buy a bomb 'off the shelf', although the Egyptian and Libyan precedents in this respect are not encouraging. Alternatively, it can try to buy weapons-grade material on the international black market, although here again the Libyan example speaks for itself. Finally, it can try to develop the relevant technology on its own, either as part of a so-called peaceful programme or as part of a clandestine effort.

Iraqi fears of Iran's nuclear intentions lay behind Iraq's air raids late in November 1987 against Iran's unfinished nuclear power plant at Bushehr. The raids followed a report on British television that Iran had been actively seeking to purchase enriched uranium from dealers in Khartoum, the capital of Sudan. The report on Channel Four, entitled 'Dispatches: The Plutonium Black Market' said Iran had tried to buy nuclear materials on the international black market. When Iraq subsequently hit Bushehr, eleven people, including a West German technician, were killed.

Iran tried to extract propaganda advantages from the attacks by claiming they would have 'the same radiological consequences as Chernobyl', but Western experts have expressed their doubts because the Bushehr plant is still far from complete.

This was not the first time that Iraq had attacked Bushehr. Indeed, the Iraqis have justified all their attacks on the nuclear power plant as legitimate revenge for Iran's 1981 bombing of Towaitha only weeks before Israel sent its war planes to finish off the job. Yet there is also a clear political message behind the Iraqi air raids — that Baghdad is keeping a watchful eye on Iran's revived interest in nuclear technology and will do its utmost to prevent Tehran from advancing its nuclear research.

An early clue to the Khomeini regime's long-term nuclear interests was the decision in 1980 to keep Iran's 15 per cent shareholding in the Rossing uranium mine in Namibia. It showed that interest in the atom did not die with the Shah.

THE SHAH'S LEGACY

Iran started a modest programme of nuclear research in 1958, when it established a nuclear research centre at Tehran University. The centre carried out research in nuclear physics, electronics, nuclear chemistry, radiobiology and medical physics.[3] Its aims were similar to those of the Iraqi Nuclear Institute established two years earlier in Baghdad. The Tehran centre came under the nominal supervision of an Atomic Energy Commission (AEC) that was part of the Ministry of Economic Affairs. A nuclear co-operation with the United States in 1957, soon after the AEC was established, was to lead to the acquisition of an experimental 5 MW research reactor for the Tehran research centre.

Iran's great leap forward in nuclear planning followed the oil-price rise of 1973, when the Shah said he intended to save oil by introducing nuclear power as an alternative source of energy. Members of the old AEC did not believe that it made economic sense for oil-rich Iran to develop nuclear power. The Shah overruled them, however. In 1974 the AEC was disbanded and the Shah founded a new Atomic Energy Organisation of Iran (AEOI) to implement an ambitious plan for installing at least 20 nuclear reactors by the end of the 1980s.[4] Orders were placed with West Germany in 1975 and with France in 1977 for the first four light-water power reactors. By the time the Shah was deposed in 1979, work on the two German reactors at

Bushehr was more than half complete. Construction had not yet begun on the two French reactors at Darkhouin.

FUEL

Iran has low-grade amounts of uranium and huge quantities are required for the nuclear power plants that the Shah anticipated would be humming with activity by the end of the century. In 1975 Iran signed an agreement to buy uranium ore from South Africa. The AEOI was also authorised to purchase a 15 per cent stake in the Rossing uranium mine in Namibia, which was being developed by Rio Tinto Zinc. A separate contract was signed with Rossing to sell Iran 1,000 tons of uranium every year for 20 years. An agreement was signed with another Southern African company, Nufcor, to buy the uranium that it processed as a by-product of its gold-mining operations. The Namibian uranium was meant to be converted into fuel for the two French reactors, which never got built, after it had been enriched at a Eurodif plant in France. Iran had acquired a stake in Eurodif via a curious route. The French and Iranian governments jointly set up a company, Sofidif, which was then allowed to acquire a 25 per cent share of Eurodif. Through this company Iran's share in Eurodif amounted to 10 per cent.

The consortium that was building the Bushehr reactors had its own arrangements to buy uranium and have it enriched in the Soviet Union before it was fabricated into fuel. A separate agreement was also reached to purchase uranium fuel from the United States. The enthusiastic Germans also agreed to train Iranian nuclear scientists at a new university that was planned for Rashd, near the Caspian Sea.

All these ambitious plans for expanding nuclear research and acquiring reactors were interrupted when the Shah was overthrown in January 1979.

NUCLEAR WEAPONS

Iran is a signatory of the NPT and the Shah justified his interest in nuclear technology as a necessary part of Iran's plan for conserving oil. Only once did he let slip his interest in weapons, later denied, when he was interviewed in 1974 by a French magazine. In response to a question about whether Iran would one day possess nuclear weapons, he reportedly said, 'Undoubtedly, and sooner than it is believed.'[5]

The Carnegie study has since disclosed that Iranian interest in lasers, which could be used for uranium enrichment, and reprocessing research at Tehran University, was evidence of a secret nuclear weapons project. The Carnegie study, citing US intelligence data, claims that the Shah also set up a nuclear weapons design team. 'Paper studies and computer analyses of nuclear weapons were under way.'[6] An Iranian nuclear engineer, now in exile in Britain, has confirmed that he took part in experiments to develop reprocessing technology. He and his colleagues had no burnt fuel to experiment with, but they conducted a 'wet run', using plain water, at a reprocessing laboratory they built at Amirabad in Tehran. The engineer, who wishes to remain anonymous, denies that these experiments were evidence of weapons research. He justifies the reprocessing experiments as part of an innocent strategy to master a complete nuclear fuel cycle.

All this was part of the Shah's legacy, which was passed on to the Khomeini regime.

OPTIONS

The revolutionary government, which earlier said it would dispense with nuclear power, has tried to revive nuclear activities in the country by opening a new research centre at Ispahan and by inviting West Germany to complete construction of the Bushehr reactors. The Germans have said that they will not resume work until the Gulf War has ended. A letter of intent was subsequently signed with the Argentine government to finish building one of the Bushehr power reactors (the other one is being used for grain storage).

Khomeini's scientists also lack the relevant infrastructure for the production of nuclear material for a weapons programme. For plutonium they would need a fuel-fabrication plant, suitable reactor (there is only the small experimental reactor at Tehran University) and reprocessing facilities. Iran, unlike other Third World threshold powers like India or Argentina, does not have the capability to produce these key components of a fuel cycle on its own. They would have to be imported from abroad, and such a move would undoubtedly attract attention.

The enrichment route is at least as difficult, and here again Tehran would have to import key technologies. The example of neighbouring Pakistan, which clandestinely imported uranium centrifuges for enrichment, does hold out some hope, although there are vast differences between the two countries. Perhaps the most important difference is that Pakistan, despite its poverty, has persuaded large numbers of highly trained scientists to stay at home and participate in the country's nuclear research programme. It is these scientists who have managed to assemble and run the centrifuge enrichment plant at Kahuta. In Iran many of the country's best scientists have left since the Shah was overthrown. The AEOI, which once had 4,500 employees, now has barely 800.

Iran's oil wealth and its access to uranium give it some bargaining power for the future. It is not inconceivable that these assets could one day be traded for the nuclear expertise of countries like Pakistan or Argentina. Relations between Tehran and Islamabad, for example, have always been close, and nuclear co-operation would further strengthen their links.

NOTES

1. *International Herald Tribune*, 14 April 1987.
2. Leonard Spector, *Going nuclear* (Carnegie Endowment, Cambridge, MA, 1987), p. 45.
3. Zdenek Cervenka and Barbara Rogers, *The nuclear axis* (Times Books, New York, 1978), p. 318.
4. US Congress, Office of Technology Assessment, *Nuclear proliferation and safeguards*, Appendix to vol. 2, part 1 (1977), p. 1.
5. Cervenka and Rogers, *The nuclear axis*, p. 332.
6. Spector, *Going nuclear*, p. 50.

8

Pakistan

Pakistan has a nuclear bomb and could assemble many more — time, circumstances and sufficient quantities of nuclear materials permitting. The dramatic admission that the international nuclear club had a ninth member (the others are widely accepted as the Great Powers, India, Israel and South Africa) was made to an Indian newspaper columnist visiting Islamabad in early 1987. His informant, the head of Pakistan's uranium-enrichment programme, Dr Abdul Qader Khan, said in his celebrated interview:[1]

> What the CIA has been saying about our possessing the bomb is correct and so is the speculation of some foreign newspapers . . . They told us that Pakistan could never produce the bomb and they doubted my capabilities, but they now know we have done it.

A few weeks later President Zia ul-Haq told an American magazine, 'You can virtually write today that Pakistan can build a [nuclear] bomb whenever it wishes. What is difficult about a bomb? Once you have acquired the technology, which Pakistan has, you can do whatever you like'.[2]

As with other countries surveyed in this book, the Pakistani search for nuclear weapons capability ostensibly began with the development of nuclear technology for peaceful purposes, but acquiring a weapons capability soon became a political objective. The unique feature of Pakistan's nuclear research has been the decision to use both plutonium-reprocessing and uranium-enrichment methods to accumulate fissile material. This decision to proceed with two parallel technologies is the product of luck and judgement. All the other countries surveyed in this book have mastered only the plutonium route. However, the Pakistan government realised in the mid-1970s that scientific advances had brought uranium enrichment within the grasp of even poorly developed countries like Pakistan.

This chapter charts the start of peaceful nuclear research in Pakistan and the subsequent, explicit change in the direction of nuclear weapons. The roles of two men, the politician Zulfikar Ali Bhutto, and the scientist Abdel Qader Khan, are of particular importance. A study of Pakistan's nuclear ambitions should logically be part of a larger study of regional rivalries with India. The two countries are deadly rivals and decisions made in one capital will often have profound follow-on effects in the other one. It is the Indian example in nuclear research — not examined in this book — that has spurred on the Pakistanis.

On the other hand, some Arab Muslim countries, for example Libya and Saudi Arabia, have ploughed money into Pakistan's nuclear programme and could reasonably expect some form of return for their early investment. For this reason Pakistan's nuclear activities have a Middle East dimension that cannot be ignored. Indeed, it could be argued that the Arab response to Israel's nuclear arming has finally found expression in the success of Pakistani scientists. How Pakistan will now help its Arab friends and allies is an issue of considerable interest.

THE EARLY EXAMPLE OF INDIA

The Indians set the pace for nuclear research in South Asia, and it was this model that the Pakistanis were to use for their own efforts. In the early years after independence there was a strong sense of rivalry between the ruling elites of the two countries that extended to every area of national activity, although in the area of nuclear research the Indians had stolen a march on their rivals. By the time the *Pakistan Atomic Energy Committee* was established in 1953, the Indians were nearly a decade ahead. Many young men and women had been sent abroad for training and there was no dearth of political support for the activities of the Indian Atomic Energy Commission.[3]

The early aims of the Pakistan Atomic Energy Committee were to survey the country for radioactive minerals and to make recommendations for a nuclear research institute in the country. Pakistan's decision to upgrade the Atomic Energy Committee to an *Atomic Energy Commission* was in direct response to a massive increase in Indian nuclear activities. The Indian intention of acquiring two experimental power reactors, and the longer-term aim of harnessing nuclear power for energy, were quickly picked up by the Pakistanis. The two men closely associated with Pakistani nuclear research in the early years were both former pupils of the famous physicist Ernest Rutherford, and had worked under him at Cambridge.

Dr R.M. Chaudhary took over as head of physics at Punjab University and his colleague, Dr Nazir Ahmad, who had been the head of a textiles research institute, became the first Chairman of the Pakistan Atomic Energy Commission. Weeks after taking over his new job he began to express sentiments that were almost identical to those of his Indian counterpart. In 1956 he told students at a nuclear physics refresher course at Punjab University:[4] 'We want to use nuclear energy in medicine and agriculture, and also for developing power for industries since we have shortages of coal and petroleum.' His immediate problem was a paucity of trained manpower, a major shortcoming that was even reflected in the composition of the Atomic Energy Commission. Apart from Ahmad, a Cambridge-trained physicist, other members of the Commission included the Agriculture Development Commissioner and the head of a medical college in Multan.[5] Ahmad's first job was to send Pakistani students abroad for further training. He started off with 14 in 1956 and the numbers rose steadily thereafter. By 1972 the country had more than 550 nuclear scientists with postgraduate qualifications.

Nuclear research expanded after the appointment of a new Chairman, Dr Ishrat Husain Usmani, another British-trained physicist. In 1958 he was appointed to the Atomic Energy Commission board by the head of the new Pakistan military government, General Ayub Khan. Two years later he was made the Chairman. Usmani, who now lives in comfortable retirement in the West, recalls he was reluctant to take the job, partly because he was no longer familiar with the subject. It was Ayub Khan who helped him make up his mind. 'You haven't forgotten how to ride a bicycle, have you?' he asked. 'Feel confident and take over.'[6]

Usmani claims that under his direction Pakistan's aims were entirely peaceful, despite increasing evidence that the Indians were trying to create military options in their own nuclear programme. It was Usmani who negotiated a $300,000 grant from the United States in 1962 to purchase a 5 MW research reactor under Eisenhower's old Atoms for Peace programme. The research reactor became the centrepiece of the new Pakistan Institute of Technology, Pinstech, for training in the nuclear sciences. The American architect Edward Stone was commissioned to design the complex, which scientists working there later described as the 'Taj Mahal of the sciences'.

In 1965 Usmani completed negotiations with Canada for a 137 MW Candu power reactor, later known by the acronym Kanupp, to provide electric power for the city of Karachi. The Canadians provided soft loans and credits of US$47 million, and the reactor was formally inaugurated in 1972. Like the 5 MW experimental reactor imported from the United States, Kanupp was placed under safeguards agreed with the International Atomic Energy Authority. Usmani defended the choice of the Candu reactor, a plutonium-producing plant, because it would enable Pakistan to make use of its own meagre resources of uranium that Pakistanis could later try fabricating into fuel. An LWR would have required enriched fuel elements — elements that Pakistan did not have the engineering skills to make on its own.[7] Less easy to justify are the early attempts to acquire laboratory-scale plutonium-reprocessing facilities from a Belgian company, Belgo Nucléaire, with which Usmani made contact in 1969.

Usmani claims he was under pressure from younger researchers at Pinstech, who wanted an opportunity to experiment with the reprocessing of nuclear materials, including plutonium, at laboratory scale. Belgo Nucléaire was willing to sign an agreement, according to Usmani, provided the quantity of reprocessed material, such as plutonium, did not exceed 'a few grams' per year. Although Usmani denies it, this early flirtation with Belgo Nucléaire was at least partly the result of scientific advances in neighbouring India, where a plutonium-reprocessing plant, designed by chemical engineers from Imperial College in London, was formally inaugurated in 1964. The Indian decision to go ahead with reprocessing technology confirmed Pakistan's worst fears that Delhi was intent on acquiring nuclear weapons. These fears were later justified when India tested a nuclear explosive in 1974.

Usmani's negotiations with the Belgians never went beyond the discussion stage. He was moved out of the Atomic Energy Commission in 1972 and it was left to his successor, Munir Ahmed Khan, a mechanical engineer with a Masters degree qualification, to finalise the agreement with the Belgians. It was also Munir who negotiated an agreement with France to build a much larger reprocessing plant at Chasma (France later withdrew from the contract under American pressure).

Munir will be best remembered for presiding over Pakistan's entry into the field of uranium-enrichment technology, hitherto the exclusive preserve of only the most highly industrialised countries in the world. The successful completion of a uranium-enrichment plant, built in total secrecy at Kahuta near Islamabad, is the key to Pakistani scientists' claims that they are now a nuclear power. As previously mentioned, two men closely associated with this success were the former Prime Minister Zulfikar Ali Bhutto and the scientist Abdul Qader Khan.

THE BHUTTO FACTOR

Credit for the expansion of Pakistan's nuclear activities was claimed by the politician Zulfikar Ali Bhutto, who served in the Ayub Khan administration and was later both Prime Minister and President in his own right. In his death-cell testimony from Rawalpindi prison in 1979, he wrote:[8]

I have been actively associated with the nuclear programme of Pakistan from October 1958 to July 1977, a span of 19 years. I was directly concerned with the subject as Foreign Minister, as Minister for Fuel, Power and Natural Resources and as Minister in charge of atomic energy. When I took charge of Pakistan's Atomic Energy Commission, it was no more than a signboard of an office. It was only a name . . . I put my entire vitality behind the task of acquiring nuclear capability for my country.

Like the Pakistani nuclear scientists, Bhutto was aware of Indian advances in nuclear research and he was anxious that Pakistan should not fall behind. The most important development in India has been the commissioning of a plutonium-reprocessing plant — entirely free of safeguards — which for the first time gives the Indians a military option in their nuclear programme. Bhutto expressed Pakistani fears a year later when he told the National Assembly in 1965, 'If India builds the bomb, we will eat grass and leaves, even go hungry. But we will get one of our own, we have no alternative.'[9]

This speech marked a turning-point in Pakistan's nuclear planning, even though important decisions had to wait until Bhutto was appointed President in 1971. He had taken the personal decision by then that Pakistan had to pursue the nuclear route and acquire a weapons capability. In an earlier set of political memoirs, published while he was out of office, Bhutto wrote:[10]

. . . it will have to be assumed that a war waged against Pakistan is capable of becoming a total war. It would be dangerous to plan for less and our plans should therefore include the nuclear deterrent . . . If Pakistan restricts or suspends her nuclear programme, it would not only enable India to blackmail Pakistan with her nuclear advantage, but would impose a crippling limitation on the development of Pakistan's science and technology.

FOREIGN ASSISTANCE

Pakistan signed a Mutual Defence Assistance Agreement with the United States in 1954 and it was to Washington that Pakistan looked for help with its nuclear research. In 1954 an Atoms for Peace exhibition touring Pakistan drew large crowds in Lahore, and a few years later it was to the United States that some of the country's aspiring nuclear scientists were sent for further training, as well as to Britain, France and Canada.

Pakistan pinned its hopes on the United States for its first experimental reactor. In 1956 the Chairman of the Atomic Energy Commission, Dr Nazir Ahmad, expressed an interest in the experimental reactor at the Massachusetts Institute of Technology, which he thought would be of a type suitable for Pakistan.[11] When that could not be arranged, his successor, Dr Usmani, negotiated the purchase of a 5 MW experimental reactor under the Atoms for Peace foreign aid programme. These were the early euphoric days of nuclear energy, and the United States and Canada were loudly advertising the benefits of the peaceful atom. Atoms for Peace, set up by the Eisenhower Administration, allowed any friendly country to apply for a United States government grant, of up to $300,000, to build a research reactor. Pakistan was the last country successfully to apply for such a grant, which led to the purchase of a research reactor from an American company, AMF.[12]

Canada was the other important country for Pakistan's nuclear needs. The Canadians were also important Commonwealth allies and in neighbouring India they had built one powerful experimental reactor, Cirus, and were in the process of negotiating the construction of two power reactors. The Canadians were susceptible to the Pakistani argument that they should be as even-handed as possible when it came to assisting India and Pakistan. It did not require much prodding for the Canadians to provide the technical expertise and soft-loan financing to build the 137 MW power reactor at Karachi, which was inaugurated in 1972. The Canadians also helped Pakistan with uranium prospecting, and in 1974 they made available an interest-free loan for a uranium fuel-fabrication plant that would make the fuel for the Kanupp reactor. Pakistan was forced to complete the fuel-fabrication plant by itself, because Canada withdrew its assistance two years later when Bhutto refused to accept safeguards on all the country's nuclear plants.

France was the third major Western power to which Pakistan turned for its nuclear needs. What the French were prepared to offer on commercial terms was a plutonium-reprocessing plant, the largest in Asia, that would give Pakistan access to all the weapons-grade material it required. An agreement for the $150 million plant was signed in 1973, but five years later the French withdrew from the contract under pressure from the Carter Administration in Washington. It was Carter's aides who had identified plutonium-reprocessing as a key technology for nuclear weapons and launched a world-wide campaign to discourage its development. Despite Pakistani protests that it had agreed to stringent IAEA safeguards for the plant at Chasma, the French insisted on bowing out.[13] Some French technicians did stay on for a year afterwards, and it is possible that they helped the Pakistanis to complete the plant.

Why did the Americans put pressure on the French to pull out of Chasma? Washington's strategy implies that Carter did not believe Pakistan's claims that it was only interested in nuclear energy for peaceful purposes. Carter's concern stemmed from the effects of the Indian nuclear test of 1974. After that took place it was hard for any outsider to believe that Pakistan would not follow suit as soon as possible.

PAKISTAN'S MOTIVES: THE ENERGY ARGUMENT

In the early 1950s Pakistani scientists shared in the world-wide euphoria about the unlimited possibilities of nuclear energy and prepared wildly over-optimistic estimates about their country's future dependence on nuclear power plants. At the 1955 UN Conference on Peaceful Uses of Atomic Energy, for instance, Pakistan predicted the installation of nearly 1100 MW of nuclear capacity by 1975.[14]

When this estimate failed to materialise, energy planners doubled their predictions to suggest even higher nuclear power consumption by the end of the century. In 1974 Munir Khan, the newly appointed Chairman of the Atomic Energy Commission, told the Pakistan Institute of Engineers that 15 nuclear power stations would be built by the end of the century. Two years later, when the oil-price hike had begun to bite, he raised the number to 24.[15]

There was nothing sinister about these estimates, although Munir, in common with other Third World energy experts, underestimated the cost of nuclear power and overestimated the pattern of energy consumption. It was Pakistan's interest in a reprocessing plant, which would make available large quantities of plutonium, that raised eyebrows in the West. It was clear even in 1973, when negotiations for the plant began with France, that such a plant could not be justified on economic grounds.

The Pakistanis used arguments deployed earlier in India that reprocessing would make plutonium available for future generations of FBRs, but the case was never a convincing one. Fast-breeders were still a long way off, even for the West, and it was premature to argue at this stage that reprocessing was a vital link along the way.

PAKISTAN'S MOTIVES: THE WEAPONS STRATEGY

Pakistan has always been sensitive about the direction of nuclear research in neighbouring India. Long before the Indian nuclear test of 1974, Pakistan had warned it would match Indian efforts in the nuclear field. Bhutto's famous 1965 speech, in which he said his countrymen would be prepared to 'eat grass' to match India's military nuclear capability, is now seen as a first warning shot to Delhi to resist the temptation to test a nuclear explosive.

The Indians, as the 1974 nuclear test demonstrated, ignored the warning. The real shock for Pakistan, however, came three years earlier. In 1971 India defeated Pakistan in a full-scale war and championed the independence of the eastern half of the country, which emerged as the sovereign state of Bangladesh. It was the shock of this defeat that crystallised Bhutto's thinking on the nuclear issue. The 1971 defeat confirmed his worst fears about India, but because it also propelled him into power, defeat enabled Bhutto to put into practice some of his own ideas about nuclear strategy. In January 1972, one month after he was appointed President, Bhutto told the country's top scientists that Pakistan was to have the nuclear bomb.

For an account of this all-important meeting, we are indebted to Bhutto's former press secretary, Khaled Hasan, who first told his 'story' on British television, and claims that he has since been hounded out of a job and forced to live in exile in Vienna.[16] There were at least 50 scientists present at the Multan meeting, which was convened in a shamiana or tent. At the end of a long and rambling speech, during which he referred to the country's humiliating defeat, Bhutto said

94

Pakistan was going to get the bomb. It was also at this meeting that Bhutto announced that he was moving Usmani out of the Atomic Energy Commission and replacing him with Munir Khan. 'I told him not to politicise the atom', Usmani recalls, 'and he knew I was for the peaceful uses of nuclear energy. But there were others who were willing to give him what he wanted.'[17] Bhutto was hardly a new convert to the advantages of nuclear weaponry. The views he expressed in Multan in 1972 were consistent with the position he had taken ten years earlier when he argued for nuclear deterrence in his book, *The myth of independence*.

The Multan speech was followed by important changes within the Atomic Energy Commission. Besides giving Munir the top job, Bhutto took personal political charge of the Commission. More scientists were sent abroad for training, and the IAEA was invited to survey Pakistan's long-term energy needs. It was on the basis of the IAEA report that Munir later announced plans for setting up 24 nuclear power plants by the end of the century. In 1973 talks began with France for a reprocessing plant to be set up at Chasma, about 150 miles southwest of Rawalpindi, and with Canada for a second nuclear power plant, Chasnupp, to be built next to the reprocessing plant. What did these expanded nuclear activities mean? Were they simply a cover for Bhutto's secret plan of diverting Pakistan's imported nuclear knowhow towards a weapons programme?

Here the Indian model is once again useful as a guide. India's nuclear research was helped along by friendly Western governments, such as Canada, who believed that they were assisting the development of a peaceful programme. That illusion was shattered, however, when Indian scientists, using Canadian-supplied research facilities, tested a nuclear explosive in May 1974. It would not have been unreasonable for a Bhutto government in Pakistan, were it to get the nuclear technology it required, to follow the Indian route. Bhutto's own public record on the nuclear weapons issue certainly lent credence to such an analysis. After the Indian nuclear test of 1974, many Western governments were convinced that this was precisely what Pakistan intended to do. The Indian test had a tremendous impact on Pakistan. Bhutto called it a 'fateful development', and he warned that if the United States did not lift its embargo on arms sales to Pakistan, Islamabad would be forced to match India's nuclear test.

Although the United States did lift the arms embargo, if only partially, Western governments remained concerned about Pakistan's nuclear intentions. This concern manifested itself most of all in reactions to Pakistan's attempts to purchase the plutonium-reprocessing plant from France. Discussions with France had begun in 1973 and an agreement to build the plant was signed in 1976. There was immediate concern in the United States, with Secretary of State Henry Kissinger reportedly threatening to make a 'horrible example' of Bhutto if he went ahead. Bhutto's Foreign Minister, Aziz Ahmed, was later to recall what Kissinger is supposed to have said. 'He told us we wouldn't know what had hit us', said Ahmed, who lost his job in the military *coup d'état*.[18]

When American threats did not work with Bhutto, Washington turned its attention to France. The French suggested a compromise by offering Pakistan a different type of reprocessing plant, a co-processing plant that would not yield plutonium, but this was unacceptable to Islamabad. In the end the French withdrew from the contract in 1978, although until the last moment Pakistan hoped France would 'honour her signature'. The Canadians exerted similar pressure on Bhutto by threatening to cut off nuclear assistance unless he gave up the reprocessing plant. When Bhutto refused, the Canadians withdrew from the fuel-fabrication plant which they were helping to set up, and they banned the export of fuel elements for the Kanupp reactor.

They were still suspicious, despite Bhutto's protests, that Pakistan was seeking a nuclear bomb capability. After all it was Bhutto himself who, despite his later disavowals, had always been hawkish on the issue, and after the Indian test it seemed inconceivable that Pakistan would not want a bomb of its own. A 1974 CIA study of nuclear weapons proliferation named Pakistan and Iran as the two countries with the strongest impulses to join the nuclear race.[19]

There were other indications of Pakistan's desperate desire for nuclear weapons status. According to one report, the Pakistanis had approached the French in 1973 with a request for information about certain types of 'mass' or 'criticality' analyses that were relevant to weapons.[20] In February 1977 there was the strange affair of Pakistani diplomats in Washington who approached an American postgraduate student, John Phillips, for access to his report — based on publicly available data — on how to make the bomb.

THE ARAB LINK

The Indian nuclear test of 1974, followed by American and Canadian attempts to block Pakistan's purchase of a reprocessing plant, represented a set-back for Bhutto, but did not prevent him from obtaining support elsewhere, from his allies in the Arab world.

Among those allies, it was the offer of financial help from Colonel Qadhafi of Libya, in return for full access to all Pakistan's nuclear research, that was the most disturbing.

Close links between Pakistan and the Arab world have been an established fact of life for nearly two decades. Many Pakistanis employed in the Middle East send home billions of dollars every year in remittances, and there is a tradition of military collaboration between Islamabad and many Arab regimes. The closest military contacts have been Saudi Arabia, where Pakistani soldiers serve on special attachment, Jordan and the Gulf States. Pakistan under Bhutto, and later under Zia, was quick to cash in on these links. Soon after his 1972 meeting with scientists in Multan, Bhutto embarked on a tour of the Islamic countries of North Africa, including Libya. After the 1973 Middle East War he visited Iran, Turkey and Saudi Arabia, and the following year Pakistan hosted an Islamic nations summit in Lahore. By 1976 Middle East government loans and grants to Pakistan were estimated at US$1 billion.[21]

Bhutto was quite prepared to use Pakistan's Islamic credentials to attract Arab funding for his nuclear programme, and he certainly hinted at the possibility before he was hanged by the military government in 1979. 'We know that Israel and South Africa have full nuclear capability', he wrote. 'The Christian, Jewish and Hindu civilisations have this capability. Only the Islamic civilisation was without it, but that position was about to change.'[22] Bhutto's boast, according to key Pakistani officials, was based on a series of key meetings held in Paris with representatives of the Libyan, Saudi and Gulf governments.

Libya's interest in the nuclear bomb has been documented in Chapter 5, and it was the Libyans who were most interested in what Pakistan had to offer. Reports of Libyan funding for Pakistan's nuclear activities first appeared in connection with the purchase of uranium from the African state of Niger. It was suggested that Libya had been underwriting the purchase of uranium ore on behalf of Pakistan.[23] These accounts were never substantiated, but a much more sinister nuclear connection between Libya and Pakistan has since been revealed.

A Pakistani chemical engineer, whose identity must be protected for personal security reasons, was present at the Paris meetings when the Libyans offered unlimited financial assistance in return for training in plutonium-reprocessing, neutronics and the handling of nuclear waste. They wanted 'full access' to the Pakistani programme. It was the revelations of this Pakistani scientist, whose identity has been revealed to the author of this book, that led television researchers

Weissman and Krosney to conclude that Bhutto intended developing an Islamic nuclear bomb. Another Pakistani official, the late Mohammed Beg, told Weissman and Krosney of Libyan couriers carrying suitcases stuffed full of US dollars for Pakistan's nuclear programme. Qadhafi, according to Beg, asked Bhutto if Libya could have the first nuclear bomb.[24]

These earlier discussions between Tripoli and Islamabad, which Pakistan denies ever took place, are now of greater significance in the light of Pakistan's nuclear bomb success. For the first time ever, Arab governments can lay claim to an assured nuclear bomb-making capability. Conservative regimes like Saudi Arabia may try to play down Pakistan's achievement, if only to discourage nuclear proliferation in the region, but they cannot deny its significance.[25] Whether Pakistan will now share its expertise with the Arab world, or whether it agrees to transfer nuclear weapons to the Middle East, is another isue — but a milestone has certainly been passed.

The route to Pakistan's nuclear bomb, however, does not run only through the plutonium-reprocessing method so avidly discussed with Qadhafi's representatives. The clever Pakistanis have acquired the fissile material for their nuclear bomb from the parallel technology of uranium-enrichment. In 1974, when negotiations for a reprocessing plant were still under way with France, the wily Mr Bhutto devised a covert strategic alternative for Pakistan. His lasting legacy, which the country's military rulers inherited, was to encourage the development of uranium-enrichment facilities in Pakistan. The five nuclear weapons powers have used both plutonium and highly enriched uranium as weapons material, but aspiring nuclear nations like India and Israel concentrated exclusively on plutonium. One of the reasons was that enriched uranium traditionally required high energy-consuming and expensive diffusion technology.

In the early 1970s the Pakistani authorities were made aware of a new and cheaper means of uranium-enrichment, the centrifuge method, perfected by scientists from the Urenco consortium of three West European nations, Britain, West Germany and Holland. This new method consists of feeding uranium hexafluoride gas, also known as hex, into centrifuges rotating at very high speeds. A centrifuge, usually about the size of a milk churn, turns the hex at such speed that lighter uranium 235 molecules are separated from heavier uranium 238 and concentrate at one end of the centrifuge. This process is repeated in a series of centrifuges, known as a cascade, until the hex is 'rich' enough to be siphoned off and restored to solid form. The amount of uranium 235 produced at Almelo was about 3 per cent, just about right for the reactor fuel that Urenco aimed to market world-wide.

To achieve weapons-grade quality, the hex would continue to circulate through the cascade until it was enriched to at least 90 per cent. Urenco scientists are banned by law from reaching these levels, but such restrictions would not apply to other countries that acquired similar technology.

PAKISTAN'S ALTERNATIVE

Pakistan's interest in enrichment dates back to 1974. One account has Bhutto's scientists asking the French if they could help with training in the new centrifuge technology being developed in Western Europe. A year later Pakistani diplomats made enquiries about purchasing centrifuge components from the Netherlands. By then a massive operation was under way to build a centrifuge enrichment plant in Pakistan, free from the prying eyes of the West, where highly enriched or weapons-grade uranium could be produced for Pakistan's rulers.

Four years later, when the reprocessing deal with France was well and truly dead, the significance of uranium-enrichment was the subject of an astonishingly frank editorial in the *Pakistan Economist*. 'Global spread of uranium-enrichment techniques makes it preferable to use uranium instead of plutonium, as it is easier to handle and offers greater design flexibility for nuclear explosives', the magazine commented. 'We conclude the reprocessing plant cannot be part of a programme for making nuclear explosives. Such a programme would be much more efficiently carried out using the uranium route than plutonium.'[26]

To run the secret enrichment programme, the Pakistani authorities were extraordinarily lucky to secure the services of a Pakistani metallurgist, Dr Abdel Qader Khan, who had worked at the Almelo Institute and was familiar with the latest developments in centrifuge enrichment. Khan, trained in West Germany and Belgium, was employed from 1972 to 1975 in Amsterdam, where he worked for FDO, a research group that did subcontracting work for Urenco. For a brief period in 1974 he had access to the 'brain box' of Almelo, where he mixed with scientists developing the centrifuge. He was also allowed to translate technical reports, one of which was classified. A subsequent Dutch government investigation identified Khan as a key figure in the Pakistani search for enrichment technology. 'It is reasonable to assume that through Dr Khan, Pakistan has been able to obtain possession of essential gas centrifuge know-how', the investigation concluded.[27]

Khan returned home to Pakistan for good in 1975, where he was appointed head of the Engineering Research Laboratories (ERL) in Rawalpindi, representing the first stage in Pakistani attempts to build their own centrifuges. Contrary to popular belief, he did not leave the Netherlands with the blueprints in his pocket, nor was he caught photographing secret manuals. Although he did write to former colleagues in Holland for details of the gas centrifuge, the service he performed for Pakistan was far more subtle. By working at Almelo, Khan was able to familiarise himself with the latest 'state of the art' technology of centrifuges. It was a priceless experience that someone like Khan, a highly trained scientist, would find invaluable.

His other great accomplishment was to compile a list of suppliers of special metals and other 'nuts and bolts' items that Urenco had used for the Almelo factory. Ever since 1976 the London Suppliers Group had restricted the export of nuclear technology, such as reprocessing and enrichment plants, that could be used for developing weapons. The list has been revised and added to since it was formulated and the Pakistanis had to make a special effort to circumvent its restrictions.

One of Khan's first jobs upon returning home was to sit down with colleagues from the newly created Special Works Organisation (SWO) and prepare a list of the parts that would have to be imported for the embryonic centrifuge plant that was being built outside Rawalpindi. SWO was able to purchase some items, like lathes, quite openly and import them into Pakistan. However, the company was concerned that the purchase of other more sensitive equipment might arouse suspicion.

From April 1977 a series of sensational media disclosures revealed the existence of dummy companies that were set up to buy the most sensitive components. They bought specialised valves from Switzerland, aluminium tubes and electric transformers from Holland and inverters, another type of high-frequency transformer, from Britain and Canada. One of the suspect companies operating in Britain was Weargate Ltd of Swansea, which bought inverters from Emerson Electronic Controls in Swindon. Emerson dispatched the inverters to Swansea and from there they were sent on to Pakistan.[28] After questions were asked in Parliament it transpired that Weargate's majority shareholder, a Mr Abdul Salam, was a college friend of Khan's. He left Britain in 1980 and set up a business in the Gulf, from where he still continues to act for Khan.[29]

It was not always necessary to use such devious methods to import parts for the three sites where centrifuges were being developed. These were the ERL laboratories near the main runway of Rawalpindi airport, the Sihala pilot plant, a few miles outside Rawalpindi, and the main plant at Kahuta, about half-way between Rawalpindi and the Indian border. Some of the items the Pakistanis wanted had not been identified for the purposes of the London Suppliers list, and in some other cases European suppliers were so anxious to fill their order books that they were pleased to provide the Pakistani authorities with whatever they wanted. One such supplier was a German engineer, Albrecht Migule, who was convicted by a West German court in 1985 of smuggling an entire plant for converting uranium powder into hex, the uranium gas that supplies the centrifuges.

Sensational media revelations about what Pakistan was hoping to achieve aroused world-wide interest in the Kahuta plant and the activities of its staff. However, attempts to see the plant, or to interview any of the staff, usually ended in disaster. In 1979 a British journalist was beaten up outside Khan's home in Islamabad, and in the same year the French ambassador to Pakistan, M. Pol le Gourrière, was assaulted on the Kahuta road. The Pakistanis were clearly sensitive about their secret installation.

THE MYSTERY OF DR KHAN

The disclosures about SWO and the secret Kahuta plant brought unwelcome publicity for Khan, and he reacted with unexpected fury. In 1979 when the *Observer* published a story entitled 'How Dr Khan stole the bomb for Islam',[30] he wrote an enraged letter to the newspaper's editor. The contents of the letter, revealed here for the first time, consisted of a tirade of filthy personal abuse. Khan described the journalists who had researched the story as 'agents' and 'bastards', and he ridiculed the notion that he was working on the trigger mechanism of a nuclear bomb. To *Der Spiegel*, the famous West German news magazine, he wrote:[31] 'Western journalism takes pride in false and malicious reporting . . . These bastards are God-appointed guardians of the world to stockpile hundreds and thousands of nuclear warheads . . . but if we start a modest programme, we are the Satans.'

In 1983, when the author of this book dared to write once again about Khan, he received another angry letter. This letter, purporting to be from one of Khan's associates, contained a familiar litany of

101

abuse. 'After all your mischief and slanderous reports, what do you expect from Dr A. Q. Khan — to lick your ass-holes and send you sweets and flowers?', the letter-writer enquired.

The reasons for such fury were not hard to find. The *Observer*'s 1979 investigation and other similar stories triggered off debates in the British and Dutch Parliaments that depicted Khan in an unflattering light. These parliamentary debates led in turn to a formal inquiry, and in 1983 a Dutch court sentenced Khan *in absentia* to four years' imprisonment for trying to obtain classified information from a former colleague at the FDO plant in the Netherlands. The sentence could not be served because Khan was safely in Pakistan and for a while the Pakistani authorities denied that they even knew of his existence. In 1985, as Khan triumphantly informed the Pakistani media, his sentence was overturned on appeal, because he had not been properly served with a summons.

It was nevertheless a victory with bitter overtones. In 1986 the Dutch Minister of Justice told Parliament that although fresh charges would not be filed against Khan, he would not be welcome if he tried to return to Holland.

USING THE MEDIA

Despite his unwelcome media attention, Khan has deliberately courted publicity, on average once in every 18 months, and used the opportunity to build himself up as a national figure. In 1984 the *Nawai Waqt* newspaper of Lahore asked him if Pakistan could make an atom bomb. Khan's reply electrified the country. 'We have the capability of doing it', he said. He added:

Although this is a political decision and my colleagues and I have no part in it, we would not disappoint the country and nation if the President were to take this extreme step for the safety and security of the country, and the job is entrusted to us.[32]

He returned to this theme a few months later when he wrote for the *Defence Journal of Karachi*:[33]

And having mastered this technology it is theoretically, and I repeat theoretically, possible for us not only to manufacture atomic bombs, but also hydrogen bombs for which only enriched uranium is used as a trigger. Indians have not got this technology or capability.

102

In 1985, in another interview with the Rawalpindi weekly *Hurmat*, Khan continued to elaborate: 'If we had to carry out this task [of making a nuclear bomb], minor difficulties may arise, but it is not at all impossible. Especially after we have successfully completed a difficult task like enrichment of uranium, this task is comparatively much easier.'[34]

What was the purpose of these interviews, including his 1987 admission to the *Observer* that Pakistan finally had its own nuclear bomb? One interpretation is that the Pakistan government was using Khan to signal its new capability to the outside world, but this is at best only a partial explanation. The latest revelations about Pakistan's nuclear efforts, published on the eve of US Senate hearings about a new aid package for Pakistan, also brought unwelcome publicity and embarrassed both the Pakistan and US governments.

The outrage in Islamabad when the interview was published was genuine enough, and Khan tried to bluster his way out of admitting responsibility. A letter he sent to the Press Council in London described the interview as 'false' and 'concocted'. Khan's protests were not believed, however. A Pakistani newspaper editor, who was present throughout the interview, confirmed its substance in a newspaper editorial the following day. Khan's former professor, Belgian metallurgist Martinus Brabers, separately confirmed that uranium was being enriched to high levels at Kahuta. Brabers visited Kahuta in November 1986 when, he said, Khan boasted that a nuclear bomb could be assembled in one month if the government gave him the go-ahead.

A far more likely explanation of Khan's bragging is his desperate desire for the recognition he believes has been denied to him. Although the Pakistan government has built him a palatial home, complete with swimming pool, and although the Kahuta plant has been officially renamed the Khan Laboratories in his honour, he feels that his place in history has not been recognised. The 1985 inteview with *Hurmat* drew attention to this apparent neglect of the great man: 'When every Tom, Dick and Harry have been honoured in Pakistan, why this indifference to A.Q. Khan?', the magazine asked.

A special function would be organised, which should be attended by the Federal Ombudsman, members of the Cabinet, chiefs of armed forces, Chief Justice of the Supreme Court, all the four governors and other dignitaries of the country, in which the President should confer on A.Q. Khan the highest award in Pakistan.[35]

Some of Khan's insecurities stem from his being an outsider. Unlike the majority of his fellow countrymen, he is a 'mohajir' or immigrant from neighbouring India. He was born in the Indian city of Bhopal in 1936, and emigrated to Pakistan 16 years later in search of a better life. 'I walked eight miles on burning sand with my suitcase on my head', he told an interviewer. 'The mischief and humiliation to which we were subjected from Ajmer to Munabao by the Hindu railway personnel, police, etc. is still vivid in my memory.'[36]

A further disadvantage for Khan in Islamic Pakistan was his decision to marry a Dutch woman, Henny, with whom he now lives in Islamabad. The extravagant praise he bestows on her in public at every given opportunity suggests Mrs Khan has not had an easy passage. 'I owe all my achievements to my begum [queen]', he told *Nawai Waqt*. 'My colleagues will bear witness that she is more Pakistani than the Pakistanis . . . she has taken Pakistani nationality. And she, as a patriot, never says bad things about Pakistan.'[37]

THE US ALLIANCE

Khan's determination to seek public acclaim for his achievements has been a source of embarrassment for Washington, which supports a new $4 billion aid package to Pakistan as a front-line state resisting Soviet expansionism in Asia. In 1981, when an earlier aid package to Pakistan was being negotiated, President Reagan persuaded Congress to waive the Symington Amendment that prohibits assistance to countries like Pakistan, known to import reprocessing or enrichment technologies. Reagan's argument was that such beefed-up assistance, which included the sale of advanced F16 fighter-bombers, would strengthen Pakistan's sense of national security and reduce the incentives for nuclear weapons.

In 1985, in the face of new evidence of Pakistan's nuclear progress, Congress passed a new amendment to the Foreign Assistance Act that made continuing aid to Pakistan conditional on the President's certifying that Islamabad did not possess a nuclear explosive. It will be much more difficult in the future to provide such a certificate.

ISLAMABAD'S EXPLANATION

Pakistani attempts to explain away the Khan interviews would be more credible but for independent evidence that the country's scientists were pursuing the development of weapons with renewed zeal. In 1984 a Pakistani national, Nazir Vaid, was deported from the United States after he was caught trying to smuggle out 50 krytrons, or electronic switches, used for detonating nuclear bombs.[38] The Vaid affair was followed by renewed speculation in Washington that China and Pakistan were co-operating in the design of nuclear warheads. Intelligence sources said two Chinese physicists had been detected at the Kahuta plant.[39] In both 1985 and 1986 Pakistan tried to buy from the West high-speed industrial cameras that are useful for designing the conventional explosive trigger of a nuclear bomb.[40]

Then, in July 1987, a suspected Pakistani agent, Arshad Pervez, was arrested in Philadelphia and accused of trying to smuggle maraging steel to Pakistan. Investigators assumed that this special-strength steel was intended for Kahuta, where it would be used in the rotors of centrifuges.

Although the Pakistan government denied all knowledge of the affair — it was described as a rogue operation — US legislators were enraged. One Congressional aide said there was a pattern of 'trying to smuggle nuclear material into Pakistan'. After the Pervez affair was disclosed, a US House of Representatives subcommittee recommended the suspension of economic aid to Pakistan for 105 days.

Western intelligence experts were able to pinpoint a weapons-design centre at Wah, 20 miles west of Islamabad, where the trigger was being assembled. It was for this site at Wah that the high-speed cameras were destined. Despite an apparent failure to buy the cameras — Pakistan may have obtained them from elsewhere — the triggers are said to have been tested at regular intervals at the top-secret Sargodha air base, headquarters of the American F16 fighters, 100 miles south of Islamabad.

Steady progress towards a weapons capability was matched in 1985 by the first stirrings in public of a nuclear bomb lobby. At a round-table discussion convened by the Lahore-based *Nawai Waqt* newspaper, a senior member of the ruling Muslim League said: 'We have learned to purify uranium. Now we should, with the help of God, produce an explosion.'[41] Similar views were expressed by other participants. They were not new, but this was the first time they had been articulated in public. They suggested the emergence of a new type of public confidence in Pakistan's nuclear capabilities.

One group not surveyed here is the military. An academic assessment of the nuclear option carried out in 1984 concluded that nuclear weapons were not attractive to professional soldiers, and pressure to get them was more likely to come from civilians.[42]

COMPLETING THE CIRCLE

Pakistan's nuclear bomb represents the culmination of a 15-year effort that had the personal political backing of the late Sulfikar Ali Bhutto. It was Bhutto who boasted that his countrymen would eat grass to keep up with India's nuclear capabilities, and later it was the ambitious Bhutto once again who set the pace for building the bomb.

Fear of India is only one ingredient in Pakistan's nuclear weapons programme, however. Pakistan's affinity with the Arab world, and the Libyan channelling of funds to Bhutto, mean Pakistan's nuclear success also has a Middle East dimension. The Israelis, who were quick to realise this, have made at least three separate overtures to India jointly to attack the nuclear plants at Pinstech and Kahuta. So far the Indians have refused, but policy could change in the future and Pakistan's nuclear bomb may yet turn out to be another fuse for lighting up the Middle East.

NOTES

1. The *Observer*, 1 March 1987.
2. *Time* magazine, 30 March 1987.
3. See, for instance, Shyam Bhatia, *India's nuclear bomb* (Vikas, New Delhi, 1979).
4. *Dawn* (Karachi), 5 June 1956.
5. *Dawn*, 9 October 1956.
6. Interview with the author, London, March 1987.
7. Ibid.
8. Zulfikar Ali Bhutto, *If I am assassinated* (Vikas, New Delhi, 1979), p. 137.
9. *Dawn*, 21 November 1965.
10. Zulfikar Ali Bhutto, *The myth of independence* (Oxford University Press, Oxford, 1969), p. 153.
11. Usmani interview.
12. Ibid.
13. See, for example, Steve Weissman and Herbert Krosney, *The Islamic bomb* (Time Books, New York, 1981), pp. 161–73.
14. Zalmay Khalilzad, 'Pakistan and the bomb', *Survival* (London) (November-December, 1979).
15. *Dawn*, 23 March 1976.
16. Interview with the author, March 1987. See also the BBC TV Panorama film *Project 706: The Islamic bomb*, 1980
17. Usmani interview.
18. Ahmed, interview with the author, Islamabad, 1979.
19. *Prospects for further proliferation of nuclear weapons*, DCI N10 1945/74, 4 September 1974.

20. Weissman and Krosney, *The Islamic bomb*, pp. 72–3.

21. Sheikh R. Ali, 'Pakistan's Islamic bomb reconsidered', *Middle East Review*, Spring 1985.

22. Bhutto, *If I am assassinated*, p. 138.

23. See, for example, the *Sunday Times*, 25 November 1979.

24. Weissman and Krosney, *The Islamic bomb*, p. 64.

25. In 1981 a *Sunday Times* report claimed Saudi Arabia had offered US$800 million to Pakistan, provided it did not allow its nuclear technology to fall into the hands of Iraq.

26. *Pakistan Economist*, 21 October 1978.

27. Cited in Sreedhar, *Pakistan's bomb* (ABC Publishing House, New Delhi, 1987).

28. The *Observer*, 9 December 1979.

29. *Financial Times*, 22 December 1980.

30. The *Observer*, 9 December 1979.

31. Weissman and Krosney, *The Islamic bomb*, p. 194.

32. Sreedhar, *Pakistan's bomb*, p. 184.

33. Ibid., pp. 234–42.

34. Ibid., pp. 289–309.

35. Ibid., p. 29.

36. Ibid., p. 237.

37. Ibid., p. 204.

38. The *Daily Telegraph*, 12 July 1985.

39. The *Guardian*, 4 August 1984.

40. *Financial Times*, 29 October 1986.

41. Leonard Spector, *Going nuclear* (Carnegie Endowment, Cambridge, MA, 1987), p. 107.

42. Stephen P. Cohen, *The Pakistan army* (University of California Press, Berkeley, 1984), pp. 155–60.

9

Conclusion

Israel has set the pace for nuclear proliferation in the Middle East. Although Israeli politicians, like the leaders of other governments surveyed in this book, have paid lip-service to the benefits of peaceful nuclear research, the real intention from the outset was to develop nuclear weapons. A secret nuclear strategy was formulated soon after the creation of Israel, when the country's first Prime Minister, David Ben Gurion, was able to secure crucial assistance from France. In the early years of this collaboration the French were given access to a new Israeli method of producing heavy water. French help with building the Dimona reactor was first revealed in 1960, when an American U2 spy plane took pictures of the site. Earlier, Ben Gurion had tried to hide the existence of the reactor by claiming it was a textiles plant.

More than 20 years later, a disgruntled Israeli technician, Mordechai Vanunu, who was kicked out of a job at Dimona, confirmed in a newspaper interview that France had also built a plutonium-reprocessing plant at Dimona. Vanunu's disclosures at the end of 1986 — before he was enticed back to Israel to stand trial — have also led Western experts to conclude that Israel has a nuclear armoury that contains upwards of 100 bombs and that some of them are thermonuclear. Furthermore, Israel's parallel development of missile technology — the Flower Project — means that Tel Aviv easily outpaces any other country in the region by the sheer sophistication of its nuclear weapons and delivery system. No Arab state can ignore this strategic reality.

Israel's nuclear programme alarmed Egypt, Tel Aviv's most powerful Arab neighbour, but Nasser and his successors were never absolutely certain if nuclear weapons had actually been produced at Dimona. This confusion was a tribute to Tel Aviv's policy of calculated ambiguity that never admitted the existence of nuclear weapons. The Egyptians' own modest efforts at acquiring nuclear technology depended initially on the Soviet Union. From 1960 onwards, when the secret of Dimona was uncovered, determined efforts were made to acquire a more powerful reactor from the West. These efforts ended in failure. Shortage of money and the effects of two Middle East wars were to blame.

There is no published evidence of Egypt's explicitly seeking nuclear weapons. One source suggests, however, that the Chinese were approached for nuclear weapons after the 1967 Middle East War. Subsequent attempts to upgrade the Inchas reactor and buy a fuel-fabrication plant and hot laboratory from French companies hint at an interest in keeping open the weapons option. Also of significance is the work of Salah Hedayat, one of the Free Officers who helped to overthrow the Egyptian monarchy. His secret efforts with Libyan backing to build a dual-purpose nuclear reactor would have given both Cairo and Tripoli access to plutonium. Moreover, Hedayat's association with the Libyans, who have a declared interest in nuclear weapons, is further circumstantial evidence that Egypt, too, had considered the nuclear military option.

The Libyans have pursued at least four different paths to developing nuclear weapons. For a brief period, with Egyptian help, they tried to build a heavy-water fuel cycle that would have yielded plutonium. Qadhafi then turned to the Chinese and tried to buy a bomb 'off the shelf'. His aides also showed interest in buying nuclear materials from the international black market, as revealed by the renegade CIA agent Edwin Wilson. Qadhafi's most successful investment, however, was in Pakistan. Libyan dollars helped to pay for Pakistan's nuclear research, which led to the assembly of at least one nuclear bomb. Relations between Tripoli and Islamabad are not as cordial as they were a decade ago, when Qadhafi promised to help Bhutto. Nevertheless, they could be revived, and a future Pakistan government — one that is short of money — may find it prudent to offer Qadhafi a return for his original investment.

President Hussein of Iraq did not admit an interest in nuclear weapons, but the pattern of his purchases from the West, including the confidential discussions with Snia Techint, would ultimately have given him a weapons capability. Iraq's subsequent abuse of the Geneva Protocol on chemical warfare does not inspire confidence in Hussein's commitment to the NPT.

Iran, Iraq's neighbour and hated enemy, also flirted with nuclear science. Both the Shah and his successors are revealed as having shown a keen interest in nuclear weapons.

The nuclear success story of Pakistan is the result of a carefully planned and clandestine effort to buy vital components of uranium centrifuges from the West. These were later re-assembled at a secret plant outside Islamabad, which has been producing highly enriched uranium for a weapons programme. Pakistan's development of nuclear weapons was motivated by a fear of neighbouring India, but Islamabad has maintained close ties with Arab countries, as well as Iran, and has sought both moral support and financial assistance from them.

Who is responsible, then, for the nuclear race now in progress in the Middle East? The temptation is to blame the Israelis: after all, they were the first to establish an Atomic Energy Commission, and Tel Aviv's desire for nuclear weapons was an established fact of life for decades. The secret research at Dimona certainly startled the Arabs and boosted nuclear research in capitals like Cairo. However, the Israelis cannot be blamed exclusively for the enhanced nuclear activities of other countries in the Middle East. All countries in the region were interested in nuclear energy and their interest was encouraged by the industrialised powers, including both the United States and the Soviet Union. The search for military options, although influenced by the example of Israel, was bound to be affected by other intra-regional disputes. The Arab-Israeli conflict, although important, was one of many in the region.

Territorial disputes between countries, such as Iraq and Kuwait, ideological rows between radical nationalists and conservatives, and Nasser's bid for regional leadership, all contributed to the volatile nature of Middle East politics. These differences were reflected in the nuclear research activities of every country in the Middle East and they held back Arab countries, for example, from pooling their resources for a joint nuclear effort.

Some earlier attempts were made to bring together Arab wealth and Arab scientific and industrial expertise for a joint programme of nuclear research. The Kuwaiti funding of the Nuclear Engineering Department at Alexandria was one example. The short-lived Egyptian-Libyan sponsorship of nuclear research was another example of regional collaboration. Such attempts, however, never lasted. Even Libya's funding of Pakistan's nuclear programme did not extend beyond Bhutto's lifetime. It was hardly surprising that an unpublished paper prepared for the Office of Technology Assessment in the United States should conclude that national rivalries in the Middle East were too strong to allow for the joint development of weapons of mass destruction.

Although industrialised countries encouraged so-called peaceful nuclear research in the Middle East, the advent of international non-proliferation measures, such as the NPT, bilateral safeguards and restrictions agreed by the London Suppliers Group, was meant to prevent the misuse of 'sensitive' nuclear technologies. In practice these measures could not be 100 per cent effective. In any case, the non-proliferation regime was assembled too late for a country like Israel, which had an advanced nuclear programme. The United States tried to impose safeguards on Dimona, but these efforts came too late and in the end were discontinued.

Pakistan accepted international inspection for some of its nuclear plants, but refused to accept comprehensive safeguards for every site in the country. The quarrel over safeguards may have delayed Islamabad's pursuit of nuclear weapons, but Pakistani scientists were ultimately successful in producing nuclear weapons material at their secret plant at Kahuta. The efficacy of non-proliferation measures could not be tested in Iraq because the Israelis, who do not believe in the NPT, bombed Towaitha. Iran, which also signed the NPT, encouraged scientists to experiment with plutonium-reprocessing, and the Shah may even have encouraged the formation of a nuclear weapons-design group. Libya has also signed the NPT, as well as accepting Soviet safeguards for the research centre at Tajora, but this has not hindered Qadhafi's secret search for nuclear weapons. Egypt has forsworn nuclear weapons but, like other countries in the region, could initiate a secret weapons-development programme in the future.

Non-proliferation measures may, therefore, delay but cannot prevent the research and development of nuclear weapons in the Middle East. The existence of age-old enmities within the Middle East, quite apart from the Arab-Israeli dispute, creates a powerful incentive to develop nuclear weapons. The nuclear race will continue until these disputes are settled and lasting political stability is achieved in the Middle East.

All this adds up to a very gloomy picture in the short and medium term. Israel will continue to bomb and blast away at any suspected Arab efforts at nuclear arming. By the same token individual Arab governments and Iran will do their best to build up independent nuclear programmes of their own. These efforts will inevitably become more secretive and renewed attempts will be made to milk the international black market for weapons grade nuclear material.

A word is appropriate at this point regarding the roles of individual scientists. Each country has thrown up an outstanding individual, or a small group of scientists, who have been at the heart of national nuclear programmes. Men like Bergmann, Hedayat, Shahristani and Khan have knowingly participated in research that could lead to the development of nuclear weapons. In the cases of Israel and Pakistan this has already happened.

It would be unfair to blame individual scientists for implementing political decisions, but they carry some responsibility for the direction of nuclear research in their own countries. Remarkably, none of the scientists from the countries surveyed has exhibited any pangs of conscience or self-doubt about the nature of his work or where it was leading. True, Shahristani was arrested for taking part in an anti-government demonstration, but this was a religious and political protest that had nothing to do with scientific research. Some Iranian nuclear scientists, disgusted by the course of the Islamic revolution, refused to work for the mullahs in Tehran. Yet the same scientists would be quite prepared to work for a regime of a different political complexion.

The absence of a conscience-stricken Oppenheimer or Sakharov is one of the saddest elements of the nuclear race in the Middle East.

Select Bibliography

Ali, Sheikh R. (1985) 'Pakistan's bomb reconsidered', *Middle East Review*, Spring

Anon. (1973) *Marketing survey for nuclear power in developing countries*, IAEA, Vienna, September

Beaton, Leonard and Maddox, John (1962) *The spread of nuclear weapons*, Chatto and Windus, London

Beckett, Brian (1976) *Israel's nuclear options*, Middle East International, London, November

Bhatia, Shyam (1979) *India's nuclear bomb*, Vikas, New Delhi

Brenner, Michael J. (1981) *Nuclear power and non-proliferation*, Cambridge University Press, Cambridge

Cervenka, Zdenek and Rogers, Barbara (1978) *The nuclear axis*, Times Books, New York

Compton, Arthur Holly (1956) *Atomic quest*, Oxford University Press, Oxford

Dunn, Lewis A. (1976) *Managing in a proliferated world*, Hudson Institute, 1 July

The Economist (1981) *Libya's nuclear dreams*, Foreign report, 9 July

El Fouly, M.E. and Snape, J.K. (1967) *Organisation for a nuclear power project*, UAR AEE Report no. 41

El Guibaily *et al.* (1971) 'Prospects of peaceful applications of nuclear explosions in the United Arab Republic', A/Conf., 49/P/144, Geneva

El Koshairy, M.A., El Guibaily *et al.*, 'Possibilities of introducing and integrating nuclear power in the Egyptian power system', A/Conf., 49/P/137, Geneva

Feldman, Shai (1982) *Israeli nuclear deterrence*, Columbia University Press, New York

Fouad, H.Y. (1974) *Optimisation of natural uranium heavy moderated reactors for salinisation*, Atomkernenergie (ATKE), Bd. 23

Hunt, S.E. (1974) *Fission, fusion and the energy crisis*, Pergamon, Oxford

Jabber, Fuad (1971) *Israel and nuclear weapons*, Chatto and Windus, London

Khalilzad, Zalmay (1979) 'Pakistan and the bomb', *Survival* (London), November-December

Lovins, Amory B. *et al.* (1980) 'Nuclear power and nuclear bombs', *Foreign Affairs*, Summer

Nader, Ralph and Abbots, John (1977) *The menace of atomic energy*, W.W. Norton, New York

Nuclear energy and nuclear proliferation, SIPRI, Taylor and Francis, London

Pry, Peter (1984) *Israel's nuclear arsenal*, Croom Helm, London

Simpson and Magrew (eds) (1984) *The international nuclear non-proliferation policy*, Macmillan, London

Spector, Leonard S. (1987) *Going nuclear*, Carnegie Endowment, Cambridge, MA

Sreedhar (1987) *Pakistan's bomb*, ABC Publishing House, New Delhi

US Congress, Office of Technology Assessment (1977) *Nuclear proliferation and safeguards*, Appendix to vol. 2, part 1

US Government (1974) *Prospects for further nuclear proliferation of nuclear weapons*, DCI N10, 1945/74, 4 September

Weissman, Steve and Krosney, Herbert (1981) *The Islamic bomb*, Times Books, New York

Index

115